THE SECRET OF

CREATING YOUR FUTURE

by TAD JAMES

Advanced Neuro Dynamics, Inc.
Honolulu, Hawaii

The Secret of Creating Your Future®
by Tad James

15 Printing

Printed in the United States of America
Editing, book design, and illustrations
by Richard Roop.

For information or free catalog, contact:

Advanced Neuro Dynamics
615 Pi'ikoi Street, Suite 501
Honolulu, Hawaii 96814 USA
(808) 596-7765 • Fax (808) 596-7764
(800) 800-MIND
e-mail: info@nlp.com
website: www.nlp.com

Library of Congress Cataloging-in-Publication Data

James, Tad.
The secret of creating your future / by Tad James.
p. cm.
1. Success- -Psychological aspects.
2. Goal (psychology)
3. Planning.
I. Title.
BF637 .S8J33 1989 158'.1- -dc20 89-61422
ISBN 0-9623272-0-4 CIP

Table of Contents

Acknowledgements

I would like to personally acknowledge all my teachers. Some of whom I met, and some whom I have not met. The most important include Maharishi Mahesh Yogi, Swami Muktananda, John Garner, Leonard Orr, Werner Erhard, Stuart Novick, Trinidad Hunt, Dana Hall, Milton Erickson, Ernest Rossi, Richard Bandler, John Grinder, Steve Andreas, Wyatt Woodsmall, Robert Klaus, Cathy Modrall, Robert Dilts, Tony Robbins, Richard Roop, and of course all my students who have taught me as much.

These people are responsible for who I am today. They gave me the information. Of course, I accepted it, so I bear at least an equivalent responsibility. I thank them all for their part.

Dedicated to the sincere seekers.
I know your path.
I'm on it too.

A WORD OF CAUTION: Even though metaphorical, the techniques described in this book are extremely powerful. It is therefore important that you use these techniques in the context for which they are presented and only for your own personal use. Basic instruction on the professional and therapeutic use of Time Line Therapy™ techniques is available in *Time Line Therapy and the Basis of Personality* by Tad James and Wyatt Woodsmall. For training in Time Line Therapy™ or Creating Your Future in your area, contact:

Advanced Neuro Dynamics
615 Pi'ikoi Street, Suite 501
Honolulu, Hawaii 96814 USA

About the Author

Everett "Tad" James is an author and a trainer. Tad has been leading personal development seminars since 1972. He has a master's degree in Communication and a Ph.D. in Ericksonian Hypnosis. He is a certified Master Trainer of Neuro Linguistic Programming (NLP). Tad is the co-author of the popular book *Time Line Therapy & The Basis of Personality,* published by Meta Publications in 1988. Tad is also a trained teacher of Transcendental Meditation and Siddha Yoga Meditation. He is the founder and chairman of Advanced Neuro Dynamics, Inc., an international training and consulting firm specializing in Human Resource Development and personal development seminars. He teaches The Secret of Creating Your Future® and other seminars throughout the United States, Canada, Europe and Australia.

Tad has a strong personal belief that within each

person is an unawakened essence, and when that essence is recognized, it begins to unfold. This belief weaves a unique pattern, not only in his style as an author, but also in his methods of coaching and consulting with individuals and businesses.

Preface

This is a story about Milon. He is a friend of mine. As I've come to know him over the years, I have seen him grow from shy, quiet, and reserved into confident, assured and competent. Today, he is extremely successful in his chosen field.

The information contained in this book is about Milon's growth. More importantly, it is about how to get results for your life in the real world — the real world where you don't have all the time you want, to do the things you know you need to do to be a success.

Use this book as a framework from which to build. Be creative and trust your instincts. There are countless ways in which you can use the powerful principles presented here. You know, far better than anyone else, what you need to do in order to get what you want.

Let us begin.

1
Milon's Secret

Milon put down his notebook and looked out the window. It was the notebook The Wizard had given him. He was so very lucky, he felt, to have the knowledge of the secret of creating the future. Not many people even knew of it in his land, and he knew that having it made him very fortunate. The endowment of actually deciding what he wanted, and then to put it out in his future was something that he found quite common these days. Not that he took the skill for granted. Most of the people in the land did not even know it was possible to create your future.

Milon saw them complaining about their lack of power in the face of Nature, events, and other people. Milon saw them giving away their power to affect their own futures as well as others' futures. He saw people riddled with guilt, fear, anxiety, and lack of self-control. He saw what he perceived to be their suffering and struggling. He knew his life was so much more comfortable than theirs, and he wondered if he could help them.

He knew that while his daily stresses were not totally eliminated, his anxiety about the future was gone, and he knew that he was in control of his life. He knew he had attained that elusive state called "self-control." You see, Milon had the capability of deciding what he wanted, and programming his future in a way so that it happened. And that was that. Whatever he wanted he was able to have.

Of course he was careful to follow the instructions to the letter. He did not deviate from them. Not one letter. Not one period, or comma. He did everything exactly as instructed. Everything he had learned so very long ago from "The Wizard." That was just one of the things that Milon was good at doing — following directions. One of the side benefits was that he had even been able to predict events in the future to a certain extent.

In his land self-control was rare. People had not always been so unrestrained in their actions, but in the last three or so generations they had lost some of the discipline that previous generations had revered so highly. This didn't bother Milon, since he was not particularly judgmental. Milon's friends, especially Glenda and Flain always commended him on his discipline. Milon did not see it as discipline, however. To him it was just knowing what he wanted, and going after it. But they saw it as something mysterious, and they wanted to know how to do it.

There was nothing mysterious about Programming Your Future, once you knew how to do it. Before you knew the processes and techniques, then perhaps, it seemed mysterious. Then, it seemed like something extremely mysterious. But after you knew how to do it, it was really quite simple.

"The Process" helped, of course: The Process — the information he had learned so very long ago from "The Wizard." That was the only name he knew. The Wizard. Sounded mysterious. Perhaps more mysterious than it needed to be. Milon had contacted the Wizard during one of his long internal journeys. Milon was fond of exploring his own internal world, and during one of those journeys, he had met the Wizard, and had been given the process for creating his own future.

While the Wizard was teaching Milon how to create his future, he gave Milon an old piece of parchment which revealed the seven frames for creating his future. The Wizard called them the seven frames:

THE SEVEN FRAMES

1. The way to have the first frame is to:

   "Take responsibility for where you are"

2. The way to have the second frame is to:

   "Clarify your Values"

3. The way to have the third frame is to:

   "Write down what you want"

4. The way to have the fourth frame is to:

   "Clean up any past memories not consistent with what you want"

5. The way to have the fifth frame is to:

   "Program your future by creating memories for your future Time Line"

6. The way to have the sixth frame is to:

   "Align your thoughts with your goals"

7. The way to have the seventh frame is to:

   "Play everything at 100%"

The Wizard then showed him how to affect his personal time record, and the universal time record, by making changes in the actual system of how his future was programmed in the Time Line. Milon remembered agonizing over the question of predestination -vs- free will before learning about the Time Line. But Milon was now certain that whatever was in his Time Line was destined to happen. He was just as certain, however, that he had total control over his Time Line, and what was in it.

Milon's friends had asked him many times to teach them about what he did with his Time Line when he was programming his future, and he wanted to, but he was not yet certain that it was something that was permitted. The Wizard had not given him permission to teach what he knew, and even though he knew his friends needed help, his integrity did not permit him to teach it to others until he had permission.

He did want to help his friends, though, since he felt very deeply for them. He loved his friends, of course, and they had become rather insistent.

Milon began to wonder if the learning that he had received from the Wizard was something that he could teach to others. He had not learned it in a way that was organized or systematic, and he knew that he had not ever thought of how to organize the material, but he knew that what he had was something that other people just had to learn. The world needed to know what Milon knew just because it made people's lives so much easier, and better.

Milon had tried so many times in the past to contact the Wizard again and get permission to share this secret with the world, but to no avail. The Wizard had not answered in quite a while. Milon was not willing to give up, however, and he decided to do something about his desire to give this technique to the world. So, he wrote a goal in the notebook the Wizard had given to him. He wrote it for one week hence, saying, "I have talked to the Wizard, and he has given me permission to teach the secret to the people of the world, so I can help them get rid of their fears, anxiety, guilt, and help them to have more self-control, so that they can have what they want in their lives, and be happy."

Then he closed his eyes, and made a picture of the goal that he had of having talked to the Wizard, and stepped into his body, and felt the feelings of having permission. Then he took the picture out to one week, made final adjustments to it, and as he inserted it into his Time Line in the future, he stepped out of his body, so he could see himself in the picture. Having done that, he looked back toward now, and noticed that the events necessary to make the event undeniable were automatically created. He then opened his eyes.

As the week wore on, Milon forgot about the programming he had done, since that was also part of the original instruction. As the time came closer and closer to the one week deadline, Milon was still confident. After all it had always worked before. But still no Wizard. As the clock ticked off the last hour up to the one week deadline, Milon sat down again and began to review what he had done, just to make sure that he had programmed his future in strict accordance with the instructions. He wanted to make sure that he had done everything right.

As he opened his notebook, as if by magic, the words appeared on the page right beneath the goal he had written:

"You alone, Milon, may proceed to share the secret of Programming Your Future with your friends. Show them how to make their lives better. Do this and I will teach you the secrets of how to become the Wizard."

2
Milon's Plan

Milon was awe-struck. He had gotten more than he had expected. Not only had he gotten the permission, but also more incentive for the future. And then he began to think about what he had done. The enormity of the project fell upon him, and he was scared. Not that fear was a foreign emotion to him, but it was so rare.

He asked himself, "Milon, what have you done. What have you asked for? What have you agreed to? Can you do it? And who are you, Milon, to do this?" His mind raced. Faster and faster. Boy, was he scared! And then he remembered the basic rule.

THE BASIC RULE

"I am in charge of my mind and therefore my results."

So he took control of his thoughts. He took a deep breath, and blew it out through his mouth, pausing with his breath fully exhaled. He remembered all the times in the past that he had succeeded. He remembered all of the times he had done exactly what he had set out to do. As he remembered his successes, one by one, he began to feel better, and better, and better. Milon knew he had to plan how to share the secret with his friends. He knew that if he did a good job the Wizard would teach him more of the secrets he wanted to know, and that would make his own life better, so he set out to figure just how to tell the world about Time Line, and Programming Your Future.

Milon determined to redo the process for himself from scratch before he set out on such an important task, and so he took responsibility for where he was. For Milon, this day was a joyous process. He knew, without a shadow of a doubt, that he himself had created this day.

He remembered the day the Wizard taught him the first frame:

"Take responsibility for where you are."

The Wizard said, "The first step to having what you want in your life, and I hesitate to say this, but I think it's important to say, the first step to having what it is that you want in your life is to take responsibility for the way your life is now. That's really important, because to the extent that you don't take responsibility for the way your life is now, you rob yourself of the power to have it be the way you want it. To the extent that you don't take responsibility, you deny your ability to have what you want in the future. So, whether or not you are responsible, act as though you are, because it gives you the power to choose how you want it to be."

As he remembered the teaching of the second frame, Milon recalled what the Wizard had said:

"Clarify your Values"
(Decide what is important to you.)

Next, Milon asked himself, "What's important about this project in the context of what I do?" As he did, he opened the notebook the Wizard had given him, and wrote at the top of the page, "VALUES: WHAT I DO," and he thought, "What's important to me about this project in the context of business, my job, or career? What's important to me about what I am doing?"

RESULTS? SECURITY?
FREEDOM?
GROWTH? SATISFACTION?
Values
FUN?
SUCCESS? INTEGRITY?
CREATIVITY? MONEY?

He wrote his values like this:

VALUES: WHAT I DO

CARER VALUES

6 CONTRIBUTION
4 A GAME WORTH PLAYING
7 RESPECT
3 IT'S INTERESTING
5 CHALLENGE
8 COMPENSATION
1 RESULTS
2 INDEPENDENCE
9 COMMUNICATION

Then he numbered the values according to their importance to him, asking himself, "Of the above values, which is the most important to me"

Then he rewrote the list of values according to their importance like this:

VALUES: WHAT I DO

CAREER VALUES
(In order of importance)

RESULTS
INDEPENDENCE
INTERESTING
A GAME WORTH PLAYING
CHALLENGE
CONTRIBUTION
RESPECT
COMPENSATION
COMMUNICATION

Milon also realized the importance of having balance in life, so he began to explore what was important to him in the other areas of his life.

Thus, he wrote about what was important to him in his personal relationships.

RELATIONSHIPS

LOVE
COMMUNICATION
MUTUAL INTEREST
FUN
LAUGHTER
CLOSENESS
CARING
FRIENDSHIP
BEAUTY

Next, he wrote about what was important to him in the area of his health and fitness.

HEALTH AND FITNESS

GOOD HEALTH
FLEXIBILITY—
BACK
LEGS
ARMS
CARDIO-VASCULAR
RANGE—
FLEXIBILITY
STABILITY
LOOKING GOOD

And personal growth.

PERSONAL GROWTH

LEARNING
EXPANSION
COMPETENCE
INTEREST
EXCITEMENT
CHALLENGE
KNOWING SOMETHING
WHICH IS NOT GENERALLY
KNOWN
GOOD TEACHERS

And his pursuit of spiritual practices.

SPIRITUALITY

THE ABILITY TO PROGRESS
RESULTS
EXPANSION OF AWARENESS
EXPERIENCE
HAVING GOOD TEACHERS
ATTAINING ONENESS
UNIVERSAL
PERSONAL
FINDING UNIVERSAL
TRUTH

Next, Milon began to look at what he wanted for the future in his project, and he remembered the Wizard's next frame:

"Write down what you want"

When the Wizard told him that, he said,"That's the next frame — to decide what you want. It is a difficult task for some people. Some people find it easy to take responsibility and discover what's important to them. But when it comes time for them to say what they want, they are not sure. You can decide what you want or you can get what you get. And, if you decide what you want, at least you will have laid out a road map for what it is that you want. Additionally, you will have given the universe instructions to produce certain results, and you can measure your progress. If you wait, age 80 is too late to decide what you want."

For just a moment Milon paused to remember the day the Wizard had given him the conditions for "Smart Goals." He remembered them as if it were today.

SMART GOALS

S

Specific

Simple

M

Measurable

Meaningful

A

All areas of life

As if now

R

Realistic

Responsible

T

Timed

Toward what you want

Milon knew that in setting his goals he needed to write goals that were simple and specifically stated.

He remembered the Wizard saying, "It is really important to be specific in setting a goal. If you want something, be specific. If you were to write a goal, `I would like to make more money,' that goal isn't specific enough. The problem is if you made one cent before the day you died, you would make more money. I can personally guarantee you that if you do nothing, you will make more money. In your land it is impossible not to make more money.

You have to be specific, because the universe will deliver what you want. That's how the universe works. You see, Milon, the universe is pure intelligence. Nature itself must be viewed as a living organism. It is purposive and it possesses deep intentionality. At its very depth, the universe acts like a processor of information. This information flows around and through all biological processes. All things are intimately and infinitely connected. Reality is not what you see, but is composed of frequencies. These frequencies can be changed, and the matter that is the universe can be affected and changed just by your attention. The universe is like your body in that respect. It will give you what you dwell upon. If you dwell on ambiguity, you will get just that. So be specific, and keep your instructions simple."

Milon remembered that his head was swimming by this time, but what the Wizard said didn't need to be remembered because just hearing it had changed his nervous system.

The Wizard continued, "The nervous system throughout the body, delivers what you tell it to deliver, and it delivers it to you in your action. It is really simple. If you have a thought in your mind, inside your head, that thought will affect your physiology and it will deliver that which you want. So you need to be specific about what you want because your body and the universe will deliver whatever it can deliver to you. If you just said, 'more money,' you might get one cent more. So what do you mean by specific? By specific, do not even say I want to make a thousand dollars more a month, or ten thousand dollars more a month. State the goal the way you want it. Say it the way you want it. Say, `I now make x number of dollars per month.' That is also measurable.

"'Measurable' goes hand in hand with specific. The reason for measurability is so that you know when you get there. Some people decide, `I want to be happy.' So does everyone, but happiness is a state. It has nothing to do with what you have.

"Also make sure that what you want is meaningful to you. Meaningful means it is yours. You want it, and so you own it. So many times, when people write goals, they don't get them. They say `I did not get it,' but if you ask them, 'Did you really want it?' you'll probably find they say, 'Not really.' Make sure you really want what you think you want.

"'Balance' is important in life. Make sure that you are not just working, but that you take time off, that you have good relationships, exercise, and the like. Make sure you plan for all areas of your life.

"Write your goals 'As if now.' When you write a goal, write it as if it were now, not in the future.

"One of the other things that is real important in setting goals is to set goals for all areas of life. That assists us in being balanced."

"'Realistic,'" said the Wizard, "simply means that given the events in your life that you can determine, it is possible that you can achieve them. But some people set goals and the way they set goals, is that they set them up in such a way that they fail. They set unrealistic goals to prove something to themselves. That is not the way to set goals. The way to set goals is to set goals that are attainable.

"'Responsible' means that your goals are good for both you and the planet. Another word would be ecological. Ecology is the study of the effects of your actions on the greater system. Responsible means ecological for you as an individual, for all parts of your life. It also means that you, yourself, are taking into account the effects on the people around you, your city, state, nation, world and universe.

"Whenever you write something that you want in

your notebook, make sure that you put a date on it. Something that is undated just sits there in your future, and you do not get any closer to it."

Finally, he said, "Make sure that you say it the way that you want it. Not the way you do not want it, but the way you want it. That's the most important."

So, Milon turned to a clean page in his notebook. He closed his eyes, and in his mind he imagined walking out into the future. In his mind, he walked out into the future on his Time Line, to ten years. Milon wanted to get in touch with the big picture first. He wanted to discover what the future would really bring. On the way back from ten years he paused at each of the major milestones to write. He would stop at the year he wanted. Stop, and look around. Then the process was easy. All he had to do was write. He wrote, and he wrote. He wrote pages and pages of goals for ten, six, three and one years, six, three and one months. And as he wrote, he made sure that the goals he was writing were "SMART."

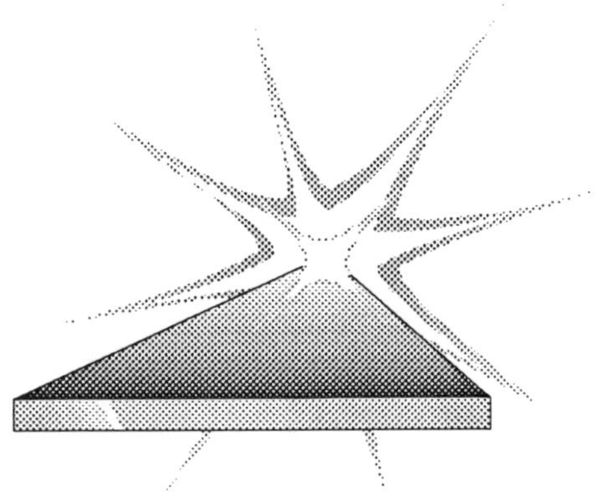

These are Milon's goals for Ten years:

GOALS FOR TEN YEARS

I HAVE BEEN MARRIED
FOR SEVEN YEARS
THE TEACHING IS NOW
WORLDWIDE
I AM MAKING Ɖ100,000
PER MONTH
WE OWN A 4 BEDROOM
HOUSE IN A NICE
AREA OF TOWN
I DRIVE A ZX003
AUTOMOBILE
I AM THE WIZARD
I AM THE AUTHOR OF
SEVERAL BOOKS

These are Milon's goals for Six years:

GOALS FOR SIX YEARS

I HAVE BEEN MARRIED
FOR THREE YEARS
THE TEACHING IS NOW
IN 17 COUNTRIES
I AM MAKING ₿60,000
PER MONTH
I HAVE JUST PURCHASED
A NEW HOME IN
A NICE AREA OF TOWN
I AM STUDYING WITH & AM
AN APPRENTICE WITH
THE WIZARD
WE ARE PLANNING A FAMILY

These are Milon's goals for Three years:

GOALS FOR THREE YEARS

I HAVE JUST BEEN
MARRIED
THE TEACHING IS SUCCESS-
FUL, WE ARE NOW
IN NINE COUNTRIES
I AM MAKING Ɖ 30,000
PER MONTH
WE ARE SAVING FOR THE
DOWNPAYMENT FOR
OUR HOUSE
THE WIZARD IS PLEASED
WITH MY WORK!

These are Milon's goals for One year:

GOALS FOR ONE YEAR

I HAVE JUST MET A
WONDERFUL
WOMAN
THE TEACHING OUTLINE IS
COMPLETE & WE
BEGIN THE TRAINING
THE WIZARD HAS
REVIEWED THE TRAINING
& APPROVED OF IT
I BEGIN TO LINE-UP THE
NETWORK FOR THE
TRAINING - WITHIN
ONE YEAR WE ARE IN
THREE COUNTRIES

These are Milon's goals for Six Months:

GOALS FOR SIX MONTHS

I AM QUITE SOCIAL NOW, MEETING A NUMBER OF EXCITING PEOPLE — THROUGH THESE CONTACTS, I WILL MEET MY WIFE & PEOPLE WHO WILL HELP ME IN THE TRAINING.

I AM LEARNING & GROWING IN THE KNOWLEDGE THAT I WILL TEACH TO OTHERS, SOON!

These are Milon's goals for Three Months:

GOALS FOR THREE MONTHS

FOR THE NEXT SIX
MONTHS, MY LIFE
WILL BE TAKEN UP
WITH PLANNING THE
TRAINING
I AM LEARNING MORE,
AND FINDING OUT
WHAT I NEED TO, TO
MAKE A DIFFERENCE
IN PEOPLE'S LIVES
WHAT I NEED TO KNOW IS
DELIVERED TO ME.

These are Milon's goals for One Month:

GOALS FOR ONE MONTH

IN THE NEXT 30 DAYS
I WILL FINISH PLANNING
OUT THE NEXT 10 YEARS
& CONCLUDE THE WORK
ON MY GOALS &
PROJECTS IN A
WAY WHICH WILL INSURE
THEIR ACCOMPLISHMENT.
ANY PROGRAM WHICH I NEED
TO TAKE, I WILL TAKE.
I WILL INVEST IN MYSELF
TO INSURE SUCCESS.

Milon remembered the Wizard, "The next frame is to clean up the past. This is one of the steps that many people leave out. It is one of the most important. If you have certain beliefs that are not supportive of what you've written that you want in the future, then you're probably not going to have what you want. Cleaning up the past, including your beliefs, attitudes, and your decisions, will help you to align the past with what it is you're deciding that you want in the present and the future."

Milon felt invigorated as he used the process that had worked so many times before, and he remembered the next frame:

"Clean up any past memories
not consistent with what you want"

He began by taking an inventory of where he was now. He asked himself, "What is my attitude on the following subjects:"

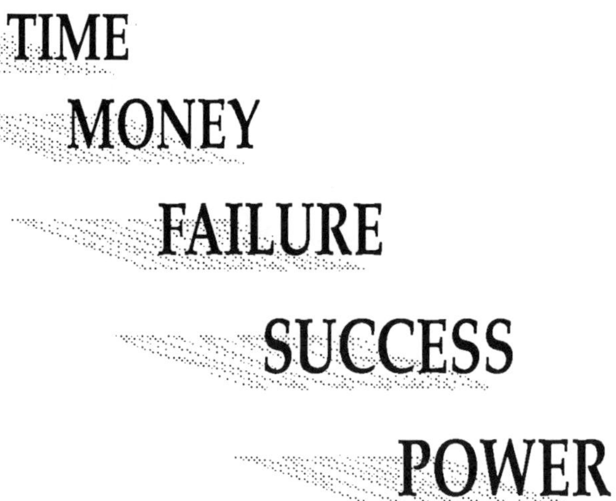

TIME

SOME PEOPLE HAVE
ENOUGH TIME; SOME
DON'T. WE ALL HAVE
ALL THE TIME THERE IS.

MONEY

MONEY IS A RESULT
OF MY BELIEFS,
DECISIONS, AND
MY THOUGHTS ABOUT
IT.

FAILURE

THERE IS NO FAILURE,
ONLY FEEDBACK.
I CANNOT FAIL, ONLY
LEARN!

SUCCESS

SUCCESS IS ASSURED
IF I FOLLOW
WHAT I KNOW
TO DO

POWER

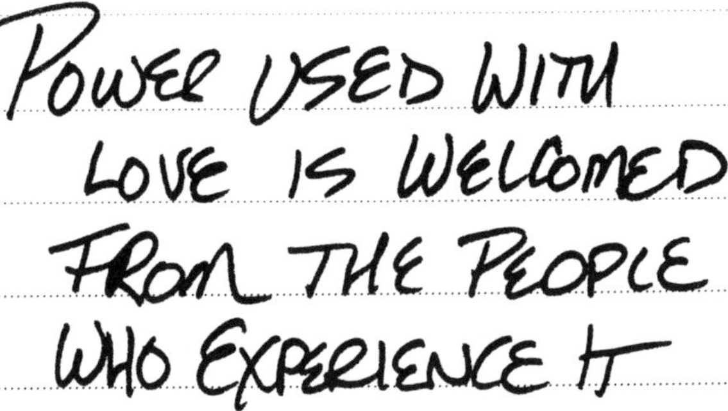

Each time he found a problem area, he asked himself, "What is the source of this problem?" and he went back on his Time Line and cleaned it up, neutralizing the negativity in that area. Milon knew that he could trust his unconscious mind to give him the information he needed to complete the process of cleaning up all of the obstacles in his past.

Milon knew that this would allow him to make sure that the next frame was easy:

"Align your thoughts with your goals"

The Wizard had said, "Where there are negative thoughts about your goals or your progress, let there be reflection to the contrary."

The Wizard had also given him an exercise to reduce the number and severity of negative thoughts. It centered around eliminating what was incomplete in his life, so he wrote down all those things that were:

STARTED, BUT NOT WORKED ON

MY DEGREE PROGRAM
MY PERSONAL GROWTH PROGRAM
REGULAR SPIRITUAL PRACTICE
WRITING TWO BOOKS
REGULAR CONCERN FOR HEALTH & FITNESS

IN PROGRESS, BUT NOT COMPLETE

MY TRAINING WITH THE WIZARD

THE PAINTING OF MY ROOM

FILING MY TAX INFORMATION

ALMOST COMPLETE, BUT STILL NOT FINISHED

ACKNOWLEDGE MY TEACHERS INCLUDING THOSE WHO WERE NOT EMPLOYED AS TEACHERS

THINGS I'VE BEEN UNABLE TO START

A FAMILY — GETTING
MARRIED — AND!!
A RELATIONSHIP
ACKNOWLEDGING MY
PARENTS — SETTING
UP COMMUNICATION

THINGS I'VE BEEN UNABLE TO CHANGE

NOTHING — I CAN
CHANGE ANYTHING IN
MY LIFE!

THINGS I'VE BEEN UNABLE TO STOP

I HAVE BEEN UNABLE
TO STOP SMOKING
CIGARETTES—
I HAVE TRIED, AND
I KNOW I NEED TO!

I ALSO NEED TO STOP
EATING JUNK FOOD!
— ESPECIALLY THE
FRIED FOODS!

When he was done with the six lists, Milon began to complete those things that were incomplete. Those things that he could complete inside himself he did. Other things required him talking to others, or writing letters. He remembered that the Wizard said, "All those things that are incomplete rob you of the power and energy to have what you want. If you can, be complete all the time."

As he completed the sixth frame, Milon began to feel the familiar feeling of exhilaration that he knew would allow him to begin to:

"Play everything at 100%"

He remembered the teaching, "Play at a hundred percent. It makes life more meaningful and fun. Holding back, not playing at a hundred percent will keep you from your goal. To the extent that you don't play at a hundred percent, you set up blocks to playing at a hundred percent. And those obstructions prevent your success. For each moment that you don't play at a hundred percent, what happens? You create a lot of barriers that are not conducive to having what you want. So play at a hundred percent. The universe supports those who play at a hundred percent. Go all out and you'll succeed. Only then can you become The Wizard.

3
The Teaching of the Time Line

Milon knew that the process he'd just gone through was dependent on its power from the Time Line, because he'd seen others in his village do all the other things that he did, and still not get the results he did, so it had to come from the Time Line. But how would he share that with the others. As he wondered, he remembered the teaching of the Wizard:

"Milon, today I am going to give you the secret of the Time Line." Milon remembered how comfortable he was with the idea now, but how he had struggled with that notion when he first heard it. The idea that people actually had inside themselves a Time Line at first seemed to him so utterly fantastic: even more fantastic that they could actually affect the Time Line to make changes in themselves and others to make their lives better.

"The Time Line is how you store your memories

Milon, it's how you know the difference between the past and the future. I have a crazy notion that if I were looking down on top of your head if this were you, Milon, and I said to you, 'Where is your past and where is your future?' that you might point to a certain direction, such as front and back or left to right or a 'v'." As Milon struggled to understand, the Wizard said, "Let us just suppose for a moment that you knew your unconscious mind could tell you how it stores your past and your future. And if you know that now, could you point to what direction your past is?"

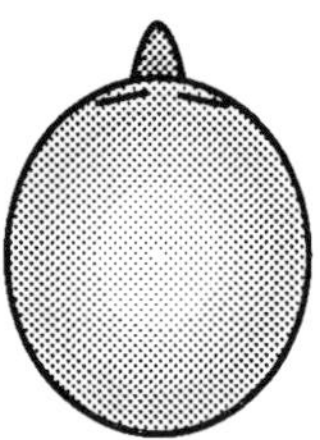

Without his even thinking about it, Milon felt his hand begin to raise up and point to the right and back.

"Very Good," said the Wizard, "and where is your future?" Again Milon felt his hand go up. This time it pointed toward the left and front. "Very good. Do you notice that the difference between your past and your future implies a line?" Milon nodded yes. "Excellent," said the Wizard. "That is your Time Line. It does not have to be a straight line but there is an implication of a line there. Do you understand?" Milon nodded yes, again.

"What I would like to ask you to do now is, if you would, could you imagine rising up above that Time Line? Could you leave the multitude that is the collection of your memories where it is and just imagine for a moment that you step above it? Just float up into the air. Way up in the air." Milon felt himself beginning to rise, and he floated up. It seemed as if his body were rising up and his memories stayed where they were and suddenly it seemed as though he was up in the air, even though he knew he was still sitting in the room. In fact, in his mind, when he looked down, he could see his Time Line below him stretched out like a line, brilliantly hanging there in space. As if from a long ways away, he heard the Wizard say, "Just go out toward the future end of your Time Line, as far out as you can." Milon nodded his head in the affirmative. "Now move into the past right back to the beginning of your Time Line." Milon nodded again. "Come right back to now, and down into now."

Milon opened his eyes. He felt as though he'd been on a long inner journey, and since this was his first time, he was surprised that it was so easy. "It was easy?" The Wizard asked, "Is that something that is easy for you to do? Did you have any trouble doing that?"

"No." Milon then asked, "when you are above your Time Line, are you supposed to be looking at yourself?" The Wizard answered, "You could be, or your self could go up and you could just be looking down on your memories of the past and of the future. What did you do?"

Milon answered, "I floated up and my memories stayed there." "Whatever you did," said the Wizard, "was perfect. I want to make sure that you have gotten this part, because it is a really important step to the process of Time Line. What we are looking for is how you organize memories. You, in fact, have a way of organizing your memories, so that you know the difference between the past and the future. Because, when you think about it, you must know the difference between the past and the future. It's very important.

"Let's say it was Tax Day." Milon knew that day. That was the day that the King collected the taxes from all the people who had made money in the previous year. Milon knew that the taxes were to help run the kingdom and keep him safe, but many times he was not sure if the taxes he paid were doing him any good!

"If you paid your taxes on Tax Day, and then you forgot, I am sure the King would find a way to collect them again from you." Milon laughed. But when he thought about it, he knew it was probably true.

The Wizard asked, "You had breakfast this morning, didn't you? How do you know you had breakfast this morning? There has to be a way that you know." Milon said, "I remember it."

"Good," said the Wizard. "Your Time Line is how you remember it. But how do you know the difference between what you remember and what you think is going to happen in the future?" Milon laughed nervously, he had never thought of that. "I am serious," said the Wizard. The Time Line is how you know. Your Time Line is how you know the difference between the past and the future.

"Can you recall a memory from age seven? And then age sixteen, and twenty three?" Milon nodded, "yes." "And now, think of something that is going to happen next week. And imagine something that is going to happen a year from now." Milon nodded. "Are those organized in a line as you recall them?" Milon nodded, "yes."

The Wizard continued, "Would you please once again get up above your Time Line and this time I would like you to float far up in the air so that you are looking down on the entire continuum of past, present and future. Now, some people like to put their eyes up because it is easier to visualize that way but still imagine gaining some distance on your Time Line. And what I would like you to do, if you can, is to be up above it so that this time you are looking down on the entire Time Line, so that you are actually looking down on the entire continuum of past, present and future."

Again Milon went way up in the air, and his memories seemed to stay right there below him where his head had been a moment before. As he looked down he could see his memories arranged below him in a line like a series of slides stretching below, and he became fascinated with the idea that all his memories were right there below him. He began to consider the possibilities. He began to wonder what he could do with Time Line, and as he looked down, his Time Line seemed only an inch long. In fact, he was so engrossed in thought that he almost missed the Wizard's next words, "Just hover over your Time Line and move easily out into the future. Very good. Go all the way out into the future, all the way out to the future end of your Time Line, and gaze in the future direction. Notice what you see as you look out toward the future.

The Wizard waited until he had done that, and then said, "Good. Now go all the way back into the past. All the way out to the past end of your Time Line, and gaze in the past direction. Notice what you see as you look out toward the past." When Milon had done that, a memory came to mind that he hadn't thought of in years, a happy memory and he smiled. Milon was thoroughly enjoying his journey on the Time Line. The Wizard said, "Come back to now, and glide down into now."

Milon once again felt as though he had been on a long trip. He was surprised to feel so rested. "Did you find that easy to do, Milon?" "Yes," said Milon, "I did." "And," said the Wizard, "You were above the memories?" "Yes," Milon said. "Did you remember something you had not remembered for some time?" asked the Wizard. "Yeah," Milon smiled. "Good. Good. That means you are doing it," said the Wizard.

The Wizard continued his teaching, and Milon listened. "Time Line is how you store time internally. Everyone has a Time Line. Most people have never been aware of it. Since you are to learn about creating your future this is the first step.

Then the Wizard took a medium sized, leather bound, purple notebook out of his bag and handed it to Milon. Milon gasped! The notebook was incredible. It felt wonderful in his hand. As Milon wondered, the Wizard said, "Open it. Turn to the first page. Draw your Time Line in there. Make a diagram, of your Time Line. This is what Milon drew:

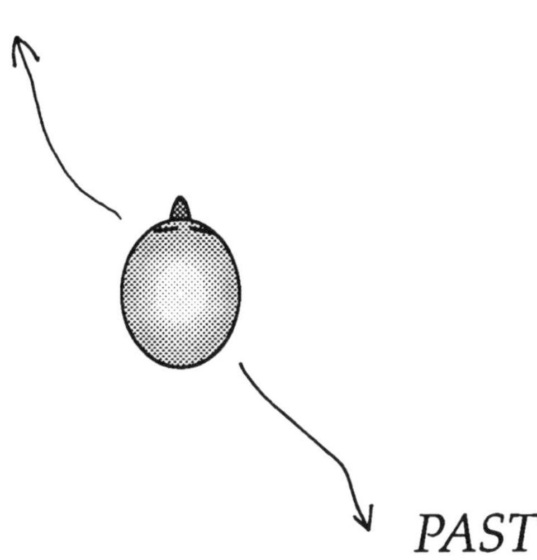

Good. Now I want you to decide what you want as a result of this training. I want you to write down one thing that you want to accomplish as a result of learning about Time Line. "Well, I have been wondering that myself," thought Milon. "Act as if you know what you want, and let your unconscious tell you what it is. You can trust your unconscious mind, you know."

So Milon closed his eyes and thought, "What do I want?" And as if by magic, his hand began to write.

I WANT TO HAVE MASTERED
ALL THE WIZARD HAS TAUGHT
& WILL TEACH ME SO I CAN
USE IT TO HELP OTHERS.

When he had finished the Wizard said, "It is important to know what you want in any situation. To be a master of Programming Your Future you must decide what it is that you want in advance. The first step is to know your outcome. Write that down." This is what Milon wrote.

FIRST STEP

Know your outcome.

"Now," the Wizard continued, "I would like you to make a picture of what you just wrote. Can you make a picture of it?" Milon nodded, "yes." Just make a picture of what it is that you wrote. Picture it in your mind's eye." Milon wondered. He had not ever been very good at picturing things in his mind, although the Time Line had been very easy. "And what I would like you to do is picture it in such a way that you know you have what you've written down. Okay?" Milon nodded, "yes." He was finding it easy to do, using Time Line. "In other words," said the Wizard, "in the picture you make, you know that you have what you wrote down. I want you to picture it in a way so that you know that you have it. If it is a process, picture it at the end of process. Picture it so you know it is complete. Does that make sense?" Milon nodded, "yes." "Good. Picture it at the end of the process. Picture it so that if you were to see that picture you would say, 'Okay, I have this.'"

Milon made a picture and pictured it in such a way that he knew that he already had what he wrote down.

"Now, make sure that you see yourself in the picture. Make sure you see your body in the picture. Take the picture with you, and get up above your Time Line. Put the picture out in the future, sometime next week, whenever it would be most appropriate for its accomplishment."

The Wizard paused while Milon took the picture out into the future.

"Glide up above your Time Line, take the picture and put it out in next week, and just sort of drop it down in there along with the other pictures that are there in the future. And as you do, notice that the events between then and now which are necessary to support making this event an undeniable occurrence are created and align themselves to support that particular goal happening automatically."

The Wizard had spoken so fast that Milon was not sure what he had said, but as the Wizard finished, Milon noticed the events in his Time Line changing and rearranging, and he wondered, "What is this?" As the rearrangement finished, the Wizard said, "When you have finished, come back to now and just descend into now."

Milon dreamily opened his eyes, "Now, was that easy for you to do," said the Wizard. "Yes?"

"Yes," Milon replied.

The Wizard said, "What we have done essentially is that we have taken one picture and put it out in your future.

"That is the teaching of how to program the Time Line for future success — how to create your future. I would like you to consider, as you went back into the past and looked at it, did you see memories back there?" "Yes," Milon said. "So think of this," the Wizard said, "what if everything that we programmed into your future were going to happen just as everything in the past is something that already happened?" Milon felt some of his old notions of how it was in the universe becoming unpinned. "That means," he said, "that there is predestination." "Well," said the Wizard, "that's true. But you have the power to decide what you want in the future. With Time Line, you can decide what is going to happen and when.

"That is the first teaching of the Time Line," the Wizard said, and with that, he was gone.

Milon continued staring out the window, contemplating what he had learned.

4
The Nature of the Universe

"But why does this all work," Milon asked the Wizard one day. "It works," replied the Wizard, "because of the nature of the universe, and the way the mind works. That's how the universe works."

Milon felt his head beginning to swim again. "What does that mean," he asked. "That means," said the Wizard, "that the nature of the universe, at its deepest level, is like your mind. There are certain principles that make Programming Your Future possible. It is an ancient teaching. In this teaching, there are five principles that make it possible for us to affect the future. Are you ready?"

"Yes!" Milon immediately sat up, grabbed his pencil and opened his notebook to a clean page, and began to write.

The Wizard said, "Here is the first principle, Milon, 'The basic nature of the universe is mind. It is pure intelligence' Milon wrote:

THE FIVE PRINCIPLES*

PRINCIPLE ONE

1. THE UNIVERSE IS MADE UP OF PURE INTELLIGENCE— ITS BASIC NATURE IS MIND.

You see, Milon, the deepest level of the universe, deeper than molecules, atoms, electrons — the deepest level of the universe — is a level where the idea of 'location' does not exist. At that level it is not possible to locate the specific position and speed of an electron. That essentially means that this deepest level pervades all that is. It has no specific location. It is omnipresent. Scientists in our world have not located it yet. In other worlds they are calling it Quantum space.

"Scientists have not been able to locate consciousness in the brain either. In fact they have no idea where consciousness is located in the human being. That is because it is like the basic Quantum level of the universe.

"Milon, the basic nature of this deepest level of the universe is consciousness — pure intelligence. At the Quantum level, at its very depth the universe acts like an information processor — like a mind. This information flows around and through all biological processes.

* *If you would like a free set of pocket cards, see appendix.*

All things are intimately and infinitely connected by the flow of the consciousness."

Milon sat and listened, awe-struck as the Wizard continued. "Nature is purposive and it possesses deep intentionality. The laws that govern the universe are contained at this Quantum level. That is why you found me here during your inner journeys. Always remember that, Milon, he who is capable of deep inner reflection will gain the secrets of the universe, because that is where they are kept."

This is what Milon wrote:

NATURE IS PURPOSIVE, AND
THE LAWS OF NATURE ARE
CONTAINED AT THE DEPTHS
OF DEEP INNER REFLECTION

The Wizard continued, "Reality is not what you see, Milon. Everything is vibrating at different rates or frequencies. Principle number two is that everything is composed of frequencies. Everything is in vibration."

Milon wrote:

PRINCIPLE TWO

2. REALITY IS NOT WHAT I SEE
IT IS VIBRATION —
— COMPOSED OF FREQUENCIES

"The difference between a rock, a tree, and a man is the difference in the rate of vibration. There is a hierarchy of vibration with matter at the low end, and energy at the higher end. Mind is even higher than energy."

"Take an object, hot or cold. That object will manifest certain heat vibrations. Those heat vibrations will, if raised, turn into light. If raised enough, a tremendous amount of power will be released, and the matter will disintegrate."

"There is the hierarchy of existence with matter at the lowest end. Sound is the next level. The vibratory rate of the sounds that man can hear is quite limited. Above sound, where the ear cannot hear, there are sounds that man cannot hear, and waves that can be transmitted, like radio waves. At higher vibratory rates sound becomes heat, then light. Above that is the level of the Quantum where dwell mind, and consciousness."

This is what Milon wrote:

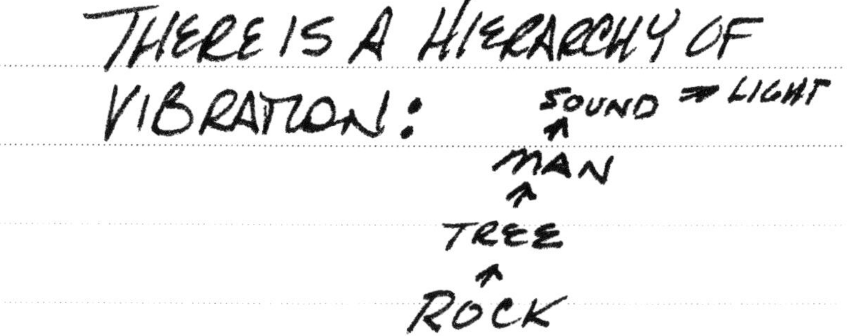

The Wizard continued, "The ancient teachings say, 'all manifestation of thought, emotion, reason, will or desire, or any mental state or condition are accompanied by vibrations.' These vibrations are, in a sense, transmitted to the area around them in the same way heat radiates outward from a hot object.

"Every thought, emotion or mental state has its corresponding rate and mode of vibration. These frequencies can be changed by a change in the thought patterns that inhabit the mind. Since the universe is also made up of vibration at the deepest level, and the matter that is the universe can be affected and changed just by your attention, the vibration of the thoughts that you are thinking may affect the very substance of the universe. The universe is like your body in that respect. It will give you what you dwell upon. If you dwell on negativity, you will get just that. Which leads us to the next principle, Milon, and that is that the universe seeks balance."

This is what Milon wrote:

PRINCIPLE THREE

3. EVERY THOUGHT OR MENTAL STATE HAS ITS OWN VIBRATION. THE UNIVERSE WILL GIVE YOU WHAT YOU DWELL UPON.

"In seeking balance, the universe will create everything with two poles. Everything has its opposite. Like has dislike, black has white, light has dark, hot has cold. But hot and cold, while different in degree are identical in context — the context of heat. The ancient saying is, 'everything is and isn't, at the same time.'

Moreover, between the poles of hot and cold, there are many degrees of hot and cold, the highest of the two being called 'warmer,' and the lower, 'colder.' There is no absolute standard for hot and cold. Nor are good and bad absolute. There are degrees of good and bad, but there is no absolute standard. These dichotomies are called the 'pairs of opposites.' The pairs of opposites are all this way, having only relative meaning."

Milon pondered the meaning of what the Wizard had said as he listened.

"Taking the first two principles together," the Wizard continued, "it is possible to change one mental state into another. Emotions and things belonging to different classes cannot be transformed into each other, but things of the same class may be transformed. So cold can become hot. Hate can become love. Fear can become courage. But hate cannot be transformed into courage.

"By changing the polarity of an emotion, through raising the mental vibrations of the energy of the emotion, we can transform it to the higher emotion. In this way, a fearful man can become a courageous man by polarizing the emotion along the line of the desired quality.

"The ancients", said the Wizard, "say, 'To change your mood or mental state, just change your vibration, through an exercise of your will, by deliberately fixing your attention on the more desirable state.' If you are sad, deliberately remember times when you were happy. You do not have to get rid of the darkness, just bring a candle into the room and the darkness will disappear."

"Do you understand?" the Wizard asked.

"Yes," Milon said.

The Wizard continued, "Good. The next Principle is closely related to the previous, in that even in the variations of the poles of opposites, there is a balance. The universe demands balance."

Milon wrote:

PRINCIPLE FOUR

4. THE UNIVERSE DEMANDS BALANCE — EVERYTHING HAS ITS OPPOSITE.

"The Law of Compensation," the Wizard said, "is that for every action, there is an equal and opposite reaction. If the pendulum swings one way, it must always swing back the other way. If you will, for a moment, stop; and consider that these swings of rhythm are also evidenced in your life. Courage is preceded by fear. Happiness and sadness oscillate.

"The ancients say, 'The man who enjoys well can also be subject to great suffering. The man who feels little pain is capable of feeling but little joy.'

"Mentally, however, it is possible to escape the low end by rising above it. This is what we do using Time Line. We are able to overcome the swing of the pendulum by making the vibrations higher and rising above the lower vibrations. In essence, we are raising the vibrations of the self above the ordinary plane of consciousness, and then simply 'refusing' to allow the pendulum of emotion and mood to swing us back.

"Even so, the Law of Compensation is operative. You will probably find that there is no such thing as an overnight success. One generally pays the price for what he wants to attain. The things that one pays a price for are always repaid.

"Do you understand," the Wizard asked.

"I do," Milon replied.

"Good. May we continue?"

"Of course," said Milon.

"Always remember, Milon, that everything is subject to the principle of cause and effect. There is a cause for every effect, and vice versa. Regardless of the thinking of late that says that there is no cause and effect, the principle is always operative."

PRINCIPLE FIVE

5. WE ARE ALWAYS COMPENSATED FOR WHAT WE DO

"If we consider cause and effect in terms of events, then strictly speaking, no one event 'creates' another event, but is merely a preceding link in the great chain of events in the day of the universe. Every thought we think, every action, every deed, creates results both directly and indirectly.

"The problem in most peoples lives is that they are

5 Take Action

"Time Line is the major component of Creating Your Future, but it's not the only thing you need to do. Of course, you must take action. In fact, that is the second step. You may want to write it down." So Milon wrote:

SECOND STEP

Take Action.

"Seems simple enough," Milon thought. "Too many people don't take action," the Wizard said. "There are essentially two tendencies. The active tendency, and the reflective tendency. People who are of the active tendency are fairly busy. They are the doers of the world. They will and do make things happen. They are pro-active. They are the people who shape the world — the entrepreneurs, the movers and shakers — the go-getters in this world. When there is something to be done, they do it. They make things happen. They create, they take initiative, and they act. While they are more likely to make mistakes, they are also more likely to do something, anything. You can tell," said the Wizard, "that I like people of the Active tendency.

"A Reactive person will not act until forced to react. Rather than being active, these people tend to study more than act. They let things take their course instead of making things happen. They prefer to study the world — the scholars in their ivory towers. A person of the Reactive tendency is a passive type of person. They often will sit back and study things because they're not ready to jump right in until they have had a chance to fully analyze them. Often they will not act until forced. They do not get things done. Stay away from them.

"Reactive persons will often do detailed studies, evaluate the consequences fully, and react only when forced, saying, 'We don't want to do anything rash!' Often, bureaucracies get caught in a reactive mode — avoiding mistakes. Things just seem to happen. Rather than being the cause, they are at the effect of events.

"Of course," the Wizard continued, "people tend to exhibit both traits. But which are you? Be sure that you are prepared to take action. Not just study it. When starting a project, Milon, make sure that you are surrounding yourself with Active people. You can find out by asking them a question. 'When you come into a situation, do you usually act quickly after sizing it up or do you do a detailed study of all the consequences, and then act?' This question has to do with predicting how much energy a person will put into pursuing their life's goals. In addition, it will predict how quickly a person will act. Size up the people you work with. Work with Active people and you will grow. Stay away from Reactive people, they will slow you down. Decide what you want, create your future using Time Line, and take action Milon."

As he read the words he had written in his notebook, Milon heard the voice of the Wizard in his left ear, "Milon, the possession of knowledge, unless expressed in action, is like the hoarding of precious metals — a vain and foolish thing. The universe demands that knowledge be used. Knowledge must be used. This is the Law of Use, there is an ancient saying, the basis of which is in use today as, 'use it or lose it.' Milon, you are on the right track, continue."

And the Wizard was gone.

Milon continued staring out the window. Contemplating what he had learned. Understanding more.

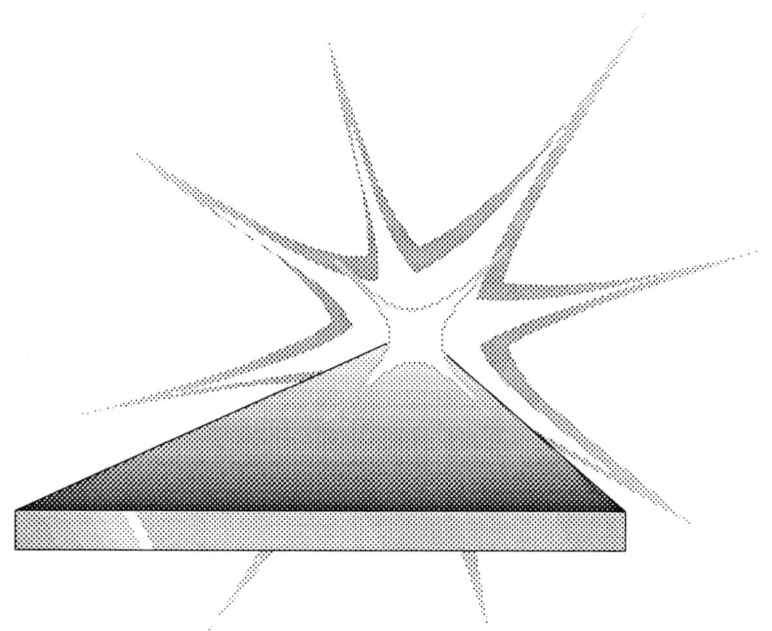

6
Time Line & Personality

The Wizard said, "Would you like to learn what the arrangement of the Time Line means in terms of a person's personality?"

"I would," said Milon. "That would be helpful for me in learning how to deal with different people. Could you tell me?"

"Listen," said the Wizard. "The Time Line that runs front to back we call "In Time," meaning essentially that you are in the Time Line or inside your experience of time. In Time people tend to be caught up in the moment. If you are an In Time person and you and I have an appointment at 2:00, you probably will not notice if I arrive at 2:05. Maybe even 2:15 you will not notice. In Time people tend to want to discover what life is and adapt to it."

"The classic organization of the Time Line of a Through Time person is left to right. The Through

Time person will have his life all laid out in advance. He pretty much knows what he wants in life. And, as opposed to the In Time person who aims to adapt to life, the Through Time person will know what he wants and will make life adapt to him.

"Now, any combination or any difference in these two Time Lines will cause a combination of In Time and Through Time personality traits." Milon realized that this was the organization of his Time Line. The Wizard continued, "So somebody who is Through Time will view time as ordered, linear, sequential, and he may carry an organizer and love it. There are people that carry the little organizers and hate them — they are In Time people. But the Through Time people carry the organizers and they love them.

"In order to plan, it helps to be Through Time. That is why when you write down your goals, you walk out on the Time Line and look around. When writing goals, set up the organization of your Time Line so that it is in front of you and crosses the room from left to right, and walk out in the future to the date and time that you are planning. Planning needs a Through Time perspective. Yet when you are working at something that you need to focus in on, if you need to be really in the moment, then that requires an In Time perspective.

"When you think of it, a long time ago, before there were factories, actually before there were clocks, there was not any need to be on time because if you and I were going to have a meeting we'd get together by the big oak tree next to the stream the third full moon after the snow melted. If I did not show up for a couple of days you would sit there and wait. You wouldn't care. You would be catching a few rabbits to eat. That was pretty much true until the Industrial Revolution. When we invented factories, we began to need people who showed up on time. Before there were factories people used to work at home. They would do piece work in their houses, or they would work somewhere, but before there were clocks there was no need to be on time. So most people were In Time in those days. Beginning with the Industrial Revolution, we began to need to be at certain places at certain times. If they opened the factory at nine o'clock and no one was there, who would catch the pieces that ran off the end and put them in boxes? Nobody. The Industrial Revolution created the need to be on time, so we created schools for our kids that started at nine o'clock, just to train the kids so they'd be on time in order to get to the factory on time. So, Through Time is an invention of modern man. Through Time is linear and sequential, much like the conveyer belt.

"Therefore, your Time Line is organized in a certain way and how your Time Line is organized will make a difference in how you experience time and how you deal with time."

"That is the second teaching of the Time Line," the Wizard said, and with that, he was gone.

Milon continued staring out the window. Contemplating what he had learned.

7 Cleaning Up the Past

"The past can be a milestone or a millstone around your neck, Milon. You can program your future, but if your past is not consistent with the future memories that you have put in your Time Line, then the results will not be as certain. Would you like to know how to clean up your past, Milon?"

"Yes," Milon said quietly. He knew that there were events and emotions in his past that were limiting his progress in the present. He had thought of this before, thinking, "If only I were different, then I would be a success."

"That's right," said the Wizard. "Let us look for a moment at your Time Line and see if there is a need to clean up some of the things that happened in the past, somewhere along the way."

"Okay," said Milon.

"What I would like to ask you to do is to, if you

would, just sort of stop, relax, take a deep breath, and just sort of rise up, way up above your Time Line, just float way up in the air." Milon nodded. "Look at the Time Line way below you and notice if, in the past or in the future, there are any dark or missing areas. The optimum is a Time Line which is contiguous. Not that it is the same brightness throughout but that there are no gaps or missing areas in your Time Line. Notice if there are gaps or missing areas." Milon stared down at his Time Line and noticed several areas below him that were different from the surrounding areas.

"Once you have noted the brightness of your Time Line, then come right back into now and organize your Time Line in the way that is most comfortable for you. And when you've done that, open your eyes."

Milon came back into the room and looked at the Wizard. "Did you find that your Time Line was of a relatively smooth coloration throughout?"

"No," said Milon. "Are there dark areas or missing areas?" asked the Wizard. "Yes," said Milon worriedly, "is that okay?" "Sure it's okay," reassured the Wizard,"Some people do have darker areas in their Time Line and some people have Time Lines that are of a relatively smooth coloration throughout. Both are common.

"A dark area in the Time Line is usually indicative of a hurt — some kind of trauma has occurred in the past. If there is a dark area in your Time Line or if there is deep hurt in your past, one of the problems is that the energy that it takes to repress that material will not go toward fully achieving what you want. When you are Programming Your Future you need to see if there are any conflicts with the goals that you have written, and the past. If there are, then you need to clean up those traumatic areas in the past.

"Typically, however, the repression of material in the past will keep a person from experiencing or being all that they can be in the future; so if there is some repressed material back there in the past it takes energy to hold those memories down so that they are not impinging on present time. When there are traumatic events in the past people pop into an emotional overlay. What happens is that the person will not be in present time but will be reacting to those previous memories. So clean up those areas in the past wherever possible.

"Milon, do you have any severe trauma back there?" "No," Milon answered. "Good," said the Wizard because if the trauma is severe, like rape or serious injury, then you shouldn't attempt to do it alone. Since it's not severe, let's proceed to clean it up. Is that all right, Milon?"*

Milon considered what it would be like to be without some of the limiting decisions of his childhood and teen years — like the horrors of his first date, or finding himself so gawky with his big teenage feet. He also remembered some of the events in the past he felt guilty about, and his fears. If that was what was preventing him from progressing then it was better to be rid of them! "Yes," he said.

"What I would like to suggest is to let us see if we can actually smooth out and clean up some of your minor rough areas in the past. Now if you have some major traumatic areas in the past, this particular process is not for you to do.

* *If severe trauma exists, this process should be handled by someone trained in Time Line Therapy™. For more information, see* Time Line Therapy & The Basis of Personality *by the author or write to the address at the front of this book.*

"If you would then, once again, would you please stop and come up above your Time Line. Just rise up above your Time Line and notice, once again, how good it feels to be above all that. Enjoy it. This time I'd like to ask you to go back to the beginning of your Time Line. Way back into the past, and staying way up above your Time Line, I would like you to go back to the beginning of your Time Line. And floating up above your Time Line, I would like you to imagine over your head now a source of infinite love and healing and I would like you to imagine that infinite source of love and healing flowing down through the top of your head and out your heart. Allow that energy, remaining infinite, to flow down through the top of your head and out through your heart and allow it to flow into your Time Line, healing the you at all the successive points in your Time Line.

"Have it flow into your Time Line and heal any of the minor traumatic events, any of the rough areas in your life, any of the times you felt unloved, or unhealed, or uncomfortable, any of the times you felt not as good as you could. As you allow the energy to flow, you can also heal any past obstacles — just allow that energy to fill them up and heal them, too.

"Notice that your Time Line becomes brighter and brighter as you do this. In fact, you may even notice that as you fill up the past, as you heal the past, that the energy can begin to flow out into the future. And if you noticed it, it is okay, just let it do that. Flow all the way out beyond now and all the way into the future, for as far as you can see. Even farther. Even farther. Even farther than that. Very good.

"When you are done with that, what I would like to ask you to do is to come forward to now, and just glide right down into now and arrange your Time Line in a way that is most comfortable. And when you have done that, go ahead and open your eyes."

Milon opened his eyes, and the room was glowing. He rubbed his eyes, and to his surprise it didn't go away. "The room looks different, doesn't it?" asked the Wizard. "Yes," Milon replied.

"Good. You are a good student." Milon was surprised. He hadn't expected such a compliment from the Wizard.

"It also may surprise you, how much more energy you have now for the future — to have what you want." The Wizard continued, "Okay, so what have we done? We have been working to clear up any past memories that could create obstacles. The main reason for that, again, is to release the energy that has been used to suppress those past traumas.

"You may have discovered that the coloration of the Time Line, the brightness, the size, whether or not the Time Line is contiguous, will give us a fair amount of information. If the Time Line is not contiguous then you are using energy which could be put in the future toward your goals. So, by healing any of the past events, that will allow more of the energy to be put toward the future. There are some other past obstacles which I would also like to clear.

"Now, as you consider the goal you have written and that we put in your future, I am wondering if you are truly aligned inside regarding the achievement of this goal. I would like you to go inside and notice if you are truly aligned with the achievement of this goal. That is, is this goal something that you truly want for yourself, and is it congruently desirable within you. Do you truly desire this particular goal? Is it something that one hundred percent of you really wants?

Milon's head was swimming again. This kind of talk was new to him. But suddenly a little voice inside of him, in his mind, said, "No," and Milon shook his head, "no."

The Wizard said, "Now if there is part of you that isn't fully in alignment with this particular goal, if part of you thinks that it isn't okay, that people like us do not get that, or if part of you says that you shouldn't get that, or can have or ought to have, I would like to suggest to that part, that were it to consider its highest intention for you, and I do not mean just its own intention, I mean its highest intention for you as a human being, as this part considers its highest intention for you, does it also see that it could, by supporting this goal, achieve its intention far more easily for you? It does, does it not?"

Milon's attention seemed to be wandering, and he shook his head to clear it. The power of the Wizard's words made his attention shift. Again, he wasn't sure what the Wizard had said, but he felt something shifting inside him. It did not make sense, but it did not need to, he felt. Inside, he heard a voice say, "Yes, okay," and he nodded, "yes."

"Very good. Excellent." The Wizard continued, "So as you consider, as the part inside you considers, this particular goal, as you consider this particular goal, do you find that the parts of your unconscious mind inside you are totally aligned and are willing to support it?"

To his surprise, Milon's head began to nod, "yes," and he smiled. That felt good.

Then the Wizard said, "That is the second way to clear up obstacles from the past — to get the alignment of all the parts of your unconscious mind." He waited for Milon to consider that and said, "Can we continue?" Milon smiled, "yes."

"The third thing I would like to suggest is that, as you consider this goal that you want, are there any decisions in your life that you have made in the past that would limit you or keep you from having this particular goal that you want?"

Milon considered as the Wizard continued, "If you were to know, if there was a limiting decision, when would it be? Are there any limiting decisions that you made in the past that would keep you from having this particular goal? Go inside right now and see if there are any limiting decisions that would keep you from having this goal. It may be a decision in your past about your ability to have or not to have what you want in your life, decisions about having money or relationships, whatever this goal is about.

"Have you found a limiting decision in your past which might limit you?" "Yes," said Milon, "doesn't everyone have one?" The Wizard replied, "Most people do, but they're not aware of them. The process here is to become aware of them and then disengage the power of that they once had. May we proceed?" Milon nodded, "yes."

"The way I would state it is, if your unconscious knew and if you could trust your unconscious mind, and I know you can, to let you know the exact moment to disconnect, which if disconnected, would allow you to be at choice regarding this particular goal that you want, to be able to choose to have it. If your unconscious mind knew, could it transport you back to the moment when you made this particular limiting decision, could you go back into the past, and just have your unconscious mind transport you instantly back to that moment."

As Milon listened, he was instantly whisked back to a childhood memory where he had rejected personal power.

"Glide down into your body at the time you made this limiting decision and I would like you to notice what emotions are present at that particular time. Would you name them silently to yourself, notice what negative emotions are there at this time in your body when you made this limiting decision."

Milon felt his body becoming overwhelmed by the negative emotions that he had felt at the time. And he grimaced.

The Wizard continued, "Come up out of that memory, it's okay. I also want you to know that there were certain positive things that you learned from this particular event, and so before we actually delete this limiting decision and the emotions that go with it, I would like to suggest that you preserve all those positive things that you learned from this event in that special place you reserve for all such learnings. And store them in there in a way that they totally support your achievement of this goal or this outcome that you have — so you have learned from this event and you can, indeed, get on with the process of having what it is that you want. Okay?"

Milon nodded, "yes."

"Having done that at the unconscious level, get up above your Time Line again, if you would, and go fifteen minutes before the beginning of the events that led to this particular event.

"Now, there may be a part of you that thinks it is important that you learned something from this event and I agree, it is important that you did learn something from this event. What I would like to suggest is that you store those learnings in that special place you reserve for all such learnings. If that part of you was aware that you had learned something from this event it would be willing to allow you to let go of those emotions, wouldn't it? Yes. So, can you store the learnings sufficiently so that you will be able to let go of those emotions? You can, can you not? And is that part willing to allow you to let go of those emotions now? It is, isn't it?"

Milon felt his head nodding.

"Now, go back before any event that led to this particular event, any event, and turn and look toward now. And as you consider those emotions, now where are those emotions?"

"Gone," Milon exclaimed.

"Very good. Excellent. So just let go of those emotions. And I would like you to also notice the decision, has the decision disappeared, also? Look and see."

Milon was amazed to feel the emotions lift off and disappear from the memory. The decision disappeared, and he smiled as he noticed the memory seemed to be clean. At least that was how it seemed to him.

"Notice how you smile. Did the emotions disappear?"

Milon nodded, "yes."

"Very good," said the Wizard. "Because there is one thing about limiting emotions and limiting decisions, they cannot stand the test of time. So when you switch the temporal perspective on them, they disappear. And what I would like to suggest is that you install in place of the decision which has disappeared, along with those emotions that have disappeared, that you install in that location, in the same time, a decision that, 'It is okay for me to have this goal or outcome that I want.' Install a decision that, 'It is okay for me to have what it is that I want when I choose to have it.'

"Would you install it in that particular memory. Just imagine making a decision that it is okay for you to 'be at choice' — to have the choice to have what you want, and install that in the memory."

The Wizard waited. "Okay?"

Milon nodded.

"Come forward to now only as quickly as you allow all of the events between then and now to re-evaluate themselves in light of your choices of having whatever it is that you want, your choice to have this particular event, this outcome that you have chosen to have. Notice that there were times in the past that you could have been at choice, but that because of the decision which you made back then, which we have just destroyed, that you had chosen not to, and this time choose to be at choice.

Milon nodded.

Milon felt his entire past changing and rearranging, he thought, "at the speed of light, it seems, or even faster, maybe at 7.57 times the speed of light. ... Wow, where did that one come from," he wondered.

"And when you get to now, come back down into now, organizing your Time Line in the way that is most comfortable for you. And when you are there, open your eyes."

Milon opened his eyes, feeling totally rearranged at the unconscious level, and he felt totally in control.

"Let us do one more thing, do you have guilt?" the Wizard asked.

"Of course," Milon replied, "everyone does. Don't they?"

"Most people do, and it keeps them from having what they want. Some people do not have guilt, and they should be guilty about that." Milon laughed. "Just kidding," said the Wizard. "He's really a good guy when you get to know him," Milon thought to himself.

"Let us look at guilt, because like limiting decisions, guilt can keep us from having those things we want. Guilt is actually a rather simple thing to handle using Time Line. We picked the more complex thing of limiting decisions first, so guilt should be easy.

"Can you think of something in the past about which you felt guilty, which as you remember it now, you can still feel the feelings of guilt?"

Milon nodded, "yes."

"Good. Can we get rid of it?"

Milon nodded.

"What I would like to ask you to do is to float up above your Time Line one more time, and go back to fifteen minutes before the beginning of the event about which you felt guilty. I would like to suggest to your unconscious mind that if there is a part of you that thinks that you should have learned something from this event, I agree. You should have learned something from this event. And so what I would like to suggest is that you store those positive learnings you should have learned from this event in that special place you reserve for all such learnings in a way that supports you in being able to have what you want in the future and not have to have this again. And if you did that, it would be okay with the part of you that is in charge of these particular learnings. It would, wouldn't it, because it would allow that part to achieve its intentions far more easily."

Milon nodded.

"Very good. Turn and look toward now, I would like you to consider this event about which you were guilty and I would like to ask you a question. Now, where's the guilt? "

To Milon's surprise it had disappeared. He told the Wizard it was gone.

"Very good. And you can just let it go. Now, the way we know that the guilt has disappeared is that you can go back and re-access the memory and it is what I call emotionally balanced, or "flat." That does not mean that you should enjoy the event. It does not mean that you should be happy about the event. But what it does mean is that you should be able to access the event and have it be emotionally balanced, or at least positive. And if you can do that, then you have, indeed, deleted the guilt from that event."

"I have," exclaimed Milon.

"Milon, guilt is the worst emotion on the planet. It truly is. I mean, what can you do about what you have already done? Yet, we are brought up to be guilty. Now, some guilt is appropriate, and should be there. But most of the guilt that people feel in our land is unnecessary. And we go through lifetimes being guilty about events that are all over and done. What can you do about something that is already done? Not much. So the problem with guilt is that it keeps one from being the magnificent human being that I know you are, Milon. So the guilts we carry hold us back from being totally unlimited. They rob energy from the future.

"Do you understand how to do it, Milon?"

"Can you review it for me again, please, so I can write it down, so I can use it in the future," asked Milon.

"The process for destroying any negative emotion, including guilt, is simple. If this is the past, this is the future, this is now," said the Wizard taking Milon's pencil and writing in his notebook, "and this is the event, the process is very simple. If you just rise up above the Time Line, glide slowly down into the event, notice what emotions are present, float up above and before the event, turn and look toward now, so you are looking across the top of the Time Line, and you notice that the guilt disappears."

This is what the Wizard wrote in Milon's notebook.

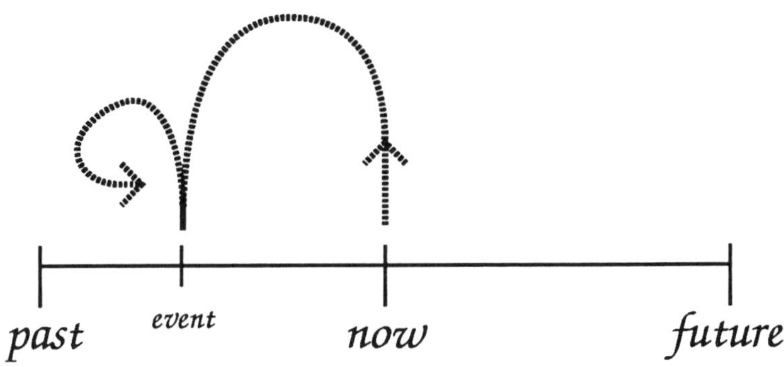

Negative Emotions

"When working with guilt just go 15 minutes before, which is what we did today. Typically people know enough about their guilt so that you do not have to have them go down into the event. They will notice it disappears. And then if you go back and re-access the event, you will notice that the guilt has disappeared. It is emotionally balanced. That is how you handle guilt."

"In the case of limiting decisions," said the Wizard writing again, "here is the future, the past and now. Let us say we have a limiting decision here. In this case the process is essentially the same, only the first step is not optional. So what you do is descend down into the event and notice what emotions are present. That is step number 1. Step number 2, back out of the event and turn and looking toward now, and you notice that the emotions disappear and that the decision disappears. So that is the process for handling a limiting decision."

This is what the Wizard wrote in Milon's notebook.

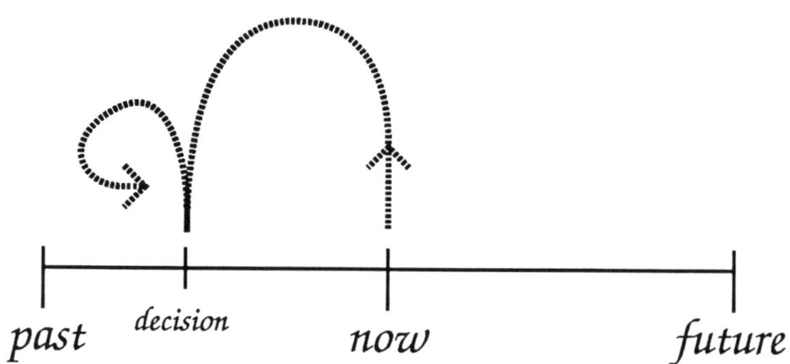

Limiting Decisions

"Do you understand, Milon?" asked the Wizard. "Yes, I do," he replied.

The Wizard continued, "The brain is usually really

quick. The mind of the human being is something that is extremely quick. By the way, these techniques are for your own personal use. This is not to be done as a therapeutic process, because there are a number of preconditions that we set up before we go out and destroy guilt for people. However, that having been done, usually the brain will make a generalization rather quickly."* *

"How about anxiety?" asked Milon.

"People who are not very good at guilt, by the way, will usually be very good at anxiety. That is what I have found anyway. People that have a lot of guilt are not very anxious, but people with anxiety do not have a lot of guilt.

"Anxiety is a lot like guilt, but in the other direction. Anxiety is an emotion of the future. Let us look at anxiety."

The Wizard took Milon's pen again, "Once again, past, future, now. There may have been anxiety in the past but typically that will not affect someone. What usually affects people is anxiety about something that is going to happen in the future. Once again, the process is the same, only in this case we go forward into the future.

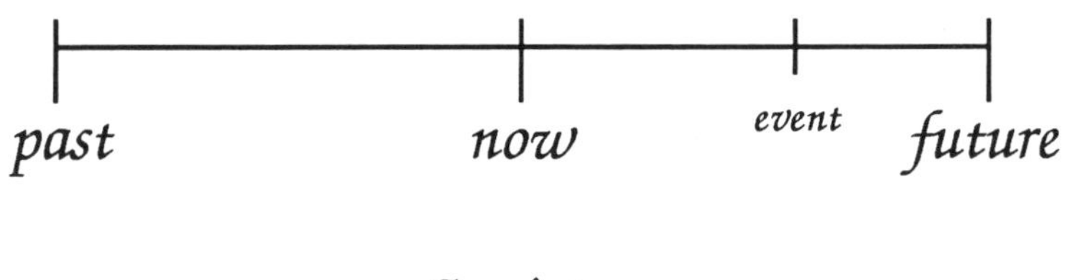

Anxiety

* * *It is important to note that any therapeutic use of these techniques should be done by someone trained in Time Line Therapy™. For more information, see* Time Line Therapy™ & The Basis of Personality *by the author.*

"Can you think of an event about which you are anxious?"

"Of course," Milon nodded.

"Could you please go forward into the future one minute after the successful completion of the event about which you are anxious?"

Milon interrupted the Wizard saying, "In the future this time, the event did not complete itself successfully. I see what I don't want!"

The Wizard said, "Why would you have something in your Time Line that was not the way you wanted it?"

Milon replied, "I do not know. Can I change it?"

"I don't know, can you?"

Milon was transported out to the event. "Yes, I can," he replied.

"Do it," said the Wizard. When Milon was done, the Wizard said, "People put stuff out in the future in their Time Line that they do not want. Now that you know the secret of Programming Your Future, you can go out into the future and look at your future Time Line and make sure that everything that is out there is something that you want to have happen to you. Okay? Do you understand, Milon?"

"Yes. Could you make me another diagram, please?"

"The process for anxiety, and we are going to do it here in a moment, is to simply go out into the future one minute past the event, and turn around and look toward now, and watch the anxiety just disappear. So, if you have something in the future about which you thought you were anxious, you know what to do."

This is what the Wizard wrote in Milon's notebook.

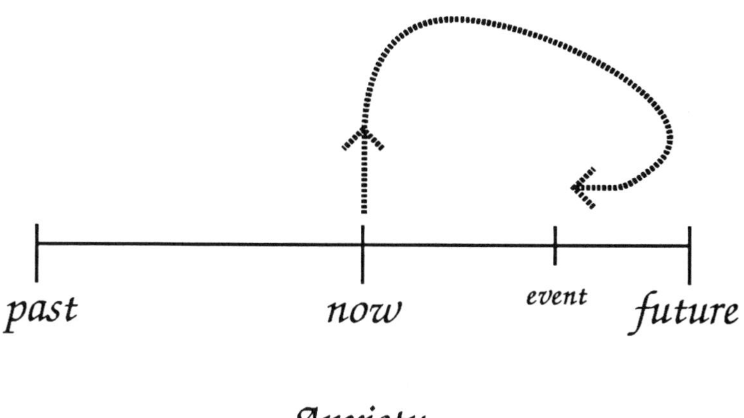

Anxiety

"Some people need anxiety to keep an edge for themselves. Some people like to use anxiety because that is what motivates them. If that is how you motivate yourself, then it probably isn't appropriate to get rid of all the anxiety that you have. But I would like to suggest that it is probably a little healthier to motivate yourself in other ways.

"The problem with anxiety as a motivator is that it tends to cause the body to not be as at ease as it could be and so anxiety tends to take its toll physiologically. So if you use anxiety to motivate yourself and were unwilling to let go of all the anxiety, my suggestion to you is that you keep the anxiety as long as it is necessary to motivate yourself until, and only until, you are ready to find other ways to motivate yourself that are more healthy for you. Is that all right, Milon?"

Milon nodded, "I let it go, and I understand."

"Here is another way to deal with anxiety," said the Wizard. "Can we play for a moment?"

"Sure," Milon replied.

"Actually shifting the position of anxiety makes a big difference in it, too. Can you remember another event about which you are anxious in the future?" Milon nodded.

"Get in touch with the physical feeling of the anxiety in your body, and as you do, notice if you can move it up just one inch? One inch up from where you feel it in your body." To Milon's surprise it changed.

Milon was trying to name the new feeling as the Wizard said, "Notice how it changes to anticipation. Now move it down an inch and notice that it is not really anxiety. In fact, many events that we thought we were anxious about, we are actually only anticipatory about. And that the location of the feeling, just by moving it slightly, will change the meaning of the event."

"Wow, I can use that," Milon thought.

"Do you understand?" the Wizard asked.

"Yes," Milon thought. And with that the Wizard was gone.

Milon continued staring out the window. Contemplating what he had learned.

8
The Nature of Prosperity

"What is the nature of prosperity?" asked Milon. "Why do some people seem to attract money, while others have so much trouble with it?"

"When people have trouble attracting money to themselves, Milon, it is because they do not understand these principles. It is often due to limited beliefs, or decisions," said the Wizard.

"What do I need to do to have money flow to me?" asked Milon.

"Understand this, Milon, it is not money that you want, it is prosperity. To cause money to flow to you is not difficult. It is only a matter of using the universal principles that you have already learned to cause the thoughts in your mind to center on the notion or idea of prosperity. You need to establish a deep understanding of the Laws of Prosperity, which I call a 'Prosperity Consciousness.'

"The Opposite is a 'Deficiency Consciousness'. A Deficiency Consciousness will inhibit the free flow of money into your life. That is not really useful for anyone. I have found that there are only a certain few beliefs that are necessary, and the Prosperity Consciousness will follow.

"Milon, this universe is an abundant universe. There is no lack of sufficiency in the universe."

Here is what Milon wrote.

PROSPERITY BELIEFS*

BELIEF ONE

1. THE UNIVERSE IS ABUNDANT.

"Next Milon, it is important to believe that the universe wants you to prosper. The universe wants to see that you have sufficiency, and that you have the abundance that you want."

"Okay," said Milon, writing the following.

BELIEF TWO

2. THE UNIVERSE WANTS ME TO PROSPER.

* *If you would like a free set of pocket cards, see appendix.*

The Wizard said, "A great man once said, 'The only thing that a man has to discover for himself is whether or not the Universe is friendly.' Look, Milon, it is, is it not?"

Milon nodded, "yes."

"It is, and it wants you to prosper. Just look around you. There's infinite abundance. There is no lack of abundance in Nature. Do you understand," the Wizard asked.

"Yes," said Milon.

"The next belief is that all prosperity begins with an idea in the mind. If the universe is pure intelligence, then it responds to your state of mind."

This is what Milon wrote.

BELIEF THREE

3. ALL PROSPERITY
BEGINS WITH AN IDEA
& THE UNIVERSE RESPONDS.

"All prosperity is first produced by the human mind. All business endeavors are built on ideas. Before the business opened its doors, before there was ANY money flowing into the business there was an idea. Any endeavor begins in the mind. So, all prosperity begins in the mind.

"If that is the case, then working harder will not produce more money, nor will working more hours produce more money. Increasing prosperity requires changing your thought processes so that they focus on prosperous thoughts. Money, and its flow into a person's life, are a direct result of the nature of the thoughts in a person's mind."

"What kind of thinking is necessary?" asked Milon.

The Wizard said, "Just affect a change in the quality of the ideas in your mind, so that the greater part of your thinking is of a prosperous nature, instead of thinking about what you lack. Bring about a change in your thoughts, and that will produce prosperity. You can change the way money behaves in your life just by changing what and how you think about it. In fact, just by holding the idea that 'The universe wants me to prosper,' just the idea of an abundant universe — a supportive universe where there is prosperity for all — will produce a 'Prosperity Consciousness.'"

"That means that you believe that there is abundance, and 'enough' for everyone, and that everyone should be prosperous. Just the idea of a sufficiency produces a sufficiency consciousness! On the other hand, thoughts of a lack of sufficiency, of a 'Deficiency Consciousness' will produce blocks (which you create) that restrict the flow of money to you.

"The human mind is infinitely powerful. The human mind, at its depth, is the same intelligence that makes up the universe. Like the universe, the mind is pure intelligence. You have that same power within you, and it is available to you. It is at your command. What keeps you from realizing your power is thinking that you don't have the power. If you believe this, then your thinking isn't in alignment with your goals, so you are less likely to get what you write down as a goal. You see, the mind always produces results exactly according to your instructions. If your thinking and goals aren't aligned, your thinking will win out.

"You're walking down the street, and perhaps you see something that you want, perhaps even something that they've written down as being a goal that you want, (like a new car), and yet, even though there's a desire there, your mind says to you, 'Oh, you can't afford that!' You've done that, haven't you?"

"Yes," Milon answered.

"That kind of thinking restricts prosperity," said the Wizard. "Here, let me use your pencil. As an analogy, the light in a light bulb might not even be enough for you to read your notebook."

This is what the Wizard drew.

"That is, if there weren't another source of light in your room. But the light in a laser has been sent to the moon and reflected back. Why? Because the light in a laser is aligned. Each ray of light is synchronized with each of the other rays in the beam of light. Like this," said the Wizard drawing.

"Without alignment of thinking, the mind is like the light bulb when it comes to your desires. The mind is filled with thoughts that aren't in alignment with actual desires, or stated desires.

"The sixth frame in Programming Your Future is to eliminate any thoughts that aren't in alignment, or don't agree, with the desired goal, outcome or state. Work on your thinking, use the universal laws, and create thoughts that will support you in having what you want.

"Do you understand," the Wizard asked.

"Yes," said Milon.

"Good. The next belief is that money is an abstraction — an abstraction of work. The value of the work you do, the amount of goods and services produced is measured abstractly by the value of money you are paid.

BELIEF FOUR

4. MONEY IS AN ABSTRACTION (OF WORK).

"If we take all the previous beliefs at face value, since all prosperity begins in the mind, and since money is an abstraction, then the greater the level of abstraction of an idea, the greater the value of that idea. As you increase the quality or abstractness of an idea, its value increases. That's why important ideas often strike us in their simplicity. It also means that as we increase the abstractness of the ideas in our mind, their value increases. The net result is an increase in our prosperity.

"Therefore, seek to increase the level of abstraction that you are capable of handling; seek to increase the level of abstraction of your thinking. Do not strive to handle more detail, delegate it. Meditation, contemplation, and affirmations are all valuable in learning how to handle abstractions. This having been mastered, your personal connection to the universal intelligence will be established, and will be bringing you new ideas that will synthesize all the specific ideas in your mind. This will generalize, leading to ideas that are more powerful, and produce more income.

"Any idea can be discussed abstractly or specifically. The range from abstract to specific is like a hierarchy. In a hierarchy, the higher an item is the more it includes — the more abstract an idea is, the more general it is and the more other specific ideas it controls. The infinite Quantum level of the universe is pure abstraction, pure intelligence. So, as you increase your mind's ability to handle abstraction you experience a greater connection to the universal intelligence. When you do, your prosperity will increase automatically.

"Is this making sense, Milon?" the Wizard asked.

"Oh yes," Milon said.

"That is good, Milon. Next, you need to understand that money has no intelligence of its own."

Milon gasped as he wrote.

BELIEF FIVE

5. MONEY HAS NO INTELLIGENCE OF ITS OWN.

The Wizard continued, "However, most people act as if money did have its own intelligence. Most people act as if money had a mind of its own. They say things like, 'Money just slips through my fingers,' or, 'Money just doesn't like me.'

"Milon, if I put a 100 coins here on top of the table, they wouldn't do anything of their own accord. They wouldn't do anything unless someone came along and did something to them! Money follows your directions exactly. It won't come to you without your direction and it won't go away from you out without your direction."

Milon wrote:

MONEY RESPONDS TO MY INSTRUCTIONS TO IT.

"The final belief is that money demands that you are aware of it at all times. This has to do with both your personal life and your business life. The key is, Milon, money demands attention on money."

BELIEF SIX

6. MONEY DEMANDS ATTENTION ON MONEY.

"You need to know where you are on a day-to-day basis. Shopkeepers in our town, for example, need to look at their income on a regular basis, perhaps as often as 2 to 3 times a week. In your life and in your business, you need to know what is going on regarding money.

"In business, Milon, 80 to 90% of the cases where a shop owner is in trouble, the shop owner does not know the financial situation. I'm not sure which comes first — lack of attention or lack of money — but they do go hand in hand. Look at your finances regularly. So, money demands attention on money: how much, where it's coming from, and where it's going!

"Do you understand?" the Wizard asked.

"Yes," Milon thought. And with that the Wizard was gone.

Milon continued staring out the window. Contemplating what he had learned.

He knew he was learning the secrets of the universe, and he felt thankful to the Wizard for sharing those secrets with him.

PROSPERITY BELIEFS

The universe is abundant

The universe wants me to prosper

All prosperity begins with an idea in mind

Money is an abstraction

Money has no intelligence of its own

Money demands attention on money

9 Grandiose Dreams

"Milon," said the Wizard, breaking into his reverie, "would you like to know how to take your goals and make them more real, more compelling, more grandiose — automate them so they happen automatically."

"Yes," said Milon, "Sure, anyone would want to be able to do that!"

"Today, Milon," said the Wizard, "I want to teach you how to have grandiose dreams. Too many people in this world have puny visions. Puny goals. They're not excited and who can blame them? Milon, if you wish to have great things, make great dreams — grandiose dreams!"

"All right," said Milon.

"If you would, make a picture of the goal that you wrote earlier. Make a picture of this particular outcome or goal that you have, and if you are not looking through your own eyes, step into your body, make sure you are looking through your own eyes, seeing what you would see, hearing what you would hear, what you would say to yourself and what others would say to you, and sensing the feelings of having this goal or outcome."

The Wizard paused as Milon did just that.

"And as you look through your own eyes, right in front of that particular goal or outcome I would like you to create the last step, so you know, 'I have it. I have my goal.'"

Milon nodded, "yes."

"Very good. Now let us adjust this picture. First, make it brighter, and brighter, so that it increases the feelings. And if you need to make it dimmer to increase the feelings, do that. Whatever makes the feelings the strongest, adjust the brightness so it does that. Adjust the size and the closeness, make it bigger and closer.

"You might try bigger and farther away, too. Whatever gives the picture the most feeling for you — adjust the size and the closeness so they are just right. Good. Now the color. Make it rich. Some people like to make it pastel, whatever makes it the most feeling for you. Enjoy the feeling of having what it is you want. Bask in it. Revel in it. Very good. Make any other adjustments you need to make to the picture, maybe some friends in there, congratulating you, or even your local newspaper writes about your accomplishment, and all your friends congratulate you. They say, 'Boy, you are the greatest!' Whatever it is that you want to add to that picture, go ahead and do it.

"Just for fun, let us play for a moment. Take that picture and project it on to a drive-in theater screen. You will have to step out of the picture so you see your body in it. Make a drive-in theater screen one hundred feet high. And as the band plays, the orchestra, the 1000 piece orchestra, plays the song, which to you, totally signifies and assures your accomplishment; notice that the air is so electric that lightning crackles over your head, just as the orchestra plays the drum roll. What an event!"

Milon's mind raced as he felt how good it feels to have what he wanted!

"Now what I would like to ask you to do, so this event is as real as it can be, take and put that event in your Time Line at the most appropriate moment for its accomplishment, a moment when its accomplishment would be undeniable to you, the moment when its accomplishment would be completely automatic. And as you put the event in the Time Line make sure you see your body in the picture and make sure you notice as you put the event in your Time Line that all the events prior to the last step are automatically created."

Milon nodded.

"And notice that all the events between then and now realign themselves and re-evaluate themselves so that the accomplishment of this event is absolute, so that the accomplishment of this event is undeniable, so that there is absolutely no way that you cannot accomplish this event as you have specified. And notice that whatever it is that you need to have this event happen the way you programmed it, is added to all the events between then and now. Do you notice that, Milon?"

Milon nodded.

"Very good. Just one more thing," the Wizard said. "Now while you are there above your Time Line, I would like you to notice if there are any resources that you personally need. Perhaps you need to learn something, or perhaps you need other resources. What I would like to ask you to consider is, has there ever been a time in the past when you had resources like that? Or, has there ever been a time in the past when you learned something easily and elegantly, in a way that surprised you that you learned so easily, and it might not have been a learning situation like in a school or anything, but you might have learned something so easily and elegantly that when it came time to say something about it, you just sort of said it automatically and you said, 'Gosh, I did not know I knew all that.' Or you may have acted in a way that further surprised you. And said, 'Gosh, did I do that? I did not know I had those resources.'

"If you could, could you go back into the past to a time like that and if there isn't one in your Time Line, imagine it from someone else's, someone you know who has those resources. And could you just go back along your Time Line into the past, float down into that event and experience the feelings of being able to learn how to have any resource that you need.

"Notice those feelings, and notice that right before you felt those feelings, there was a process that your unconscious mind was going through and the process that your unconscious mind was going through was the process that allowed you to have those feelings occur. And what your unconscious mind did was it organized completely and efficiently all the information that you had up to that point in ways that would allow you to use that information effortlessly and easily anytime in the future.

"Your unconscious mind can do that. In fact, it already has done it more than once, and you may even know that it has. And so I would like to ask that your unconscious mind pick up the process and that you wrap the feelings of being able to have any resource that you need around your body and rise up above your Time Line once again and go out into the future to this event that we have installed. Glide right down into that event and install the unconscious process, that is, the unconscious mind organizing easily and effortlessly any of the resources that you needed to have to accomplish this event. Allow the process to be installed prior to the accomplishment of this particular outcome. And allow the feelings to be attached to the picture of the goal or outcome, so that you sense them and you know you have those capabilities now. Very good. Very good. So, if you would, come back to now, and organize your Time Line in the way that is most comfortable, floating down into now, and when you are ready, go ahead and open your eyes."

As Milon came back to now, his mind raced, "Amazing. I can have whatever I want, be whomever I want to be." As he thought that thought his eyes filled with tears of gratitude for the Wizard. "Thank-you. I understand," he thought.

And the Wizard was gone.

Milon continued staring out the window. Contemplating what he had learned.

10
Milon Discovers His Life's Purpose

"I have done all you have asked so far," said Milon one day. "But where is this all leading? I mean where have we come from, and where are we going in this life? Above all, why are we here?" This was the first time Milon had dared to ask those questions, even of himself. Most of the time, questions like that made his head spin, and Milon was more of a "thinker" than most of the people in the land.

The Wizard smiled, "Finally, Milon, it is time to take up the unanswerable question, isn't it?"

Milon knew that to ask about one's purpose was a common question. But it was a question that, while common, was usually not answered. Not in one's short life, anyway, and he wondered if the Wizard was going to answer the final question.

"It is time, Milon," the Wizard said, "to take up the question of your purpose in life." The Wizard paused waiting for Milon to fully consider the last statement. "As you know, most people never get to this stage in asking about their purpose. If they do, the quest is often hard, Milon. There is a process that makes it easy for a person to discover his or her purpose, Milon, and that is with the Time Line. You are ready, Milon, otherwise you would not have asked."

Milon shivered in anticipation, and nodded, "Yes."

The Wizard said, "Good, let us proceed."

Milon closed his eyes.

This is what the Wizard said, "As we go on our journey today, we may go way high up in the air to the stars. We may go down into the depths of the earth, or into the depths of your personality. We may go forward in time in the far distant future, as far as you can see, we may go back into the past, all the way to the beginning of time. And as we go together, you and I, my voice will go with you. My voice will become the tinkling of the bells as the wind whistles through the wind chimes. My voice will become the voice of your parents or your friends, or anyone it needs to be to be consistent with your experience today. As we go on this journey, my voice will become the sounds that it needs to become, for you to have the experience internally that you need to have, as we move the sands of time. That's right, just like that, Milon.

"As you prepare, Milon, I'd like you to place a flag in now. Put a nice big flag of a color that you enjoy and put it in now. And I'd like you to tie a string to your big toe. And as you do, taking that string put the other end in your Time Line in a place that's most appropriate for you. Good.

"Now what I'd like you to do, is I'd like you to float way up above your Time Line and this time we'll make the journey together. I will go with you. This time I'd like you to move out into the future. All the way out into the future. Even farther. Right out to the future end of your Time Line. Good. Now, go even farther, past the future end of your Time Line — forward into the future. Look out to the future. Do you see the white light?"

"Yes," Milon responded dreamily, and it seemed as if his own voice was coming from a million miles away. "But it seems as if I am seeing the white light through the end of a long tunnel."

"That's right, it does, Milon. That is right. Go through the tunnel."

Milon began to move forward. Into the tunnel. As he moved through the tunnel, he saw lights all around him. He saw flashes of light and heard strange sounds, but he wasn't afraid.

"Go through the tunnel, and into the white light."

Milon shuddered as his body hit the white light.

"Become one with the white light," said the Wizard.

Milon's body disappeared, and he was free! Pure consciousness suspended in space.

From a long way away, he heard the Wizard continue, "Notice how the white light totally permeates your body, and you become as if one with the entire light. The light becomes one with you so that every inch of your body, every pore in your body, every molecule in your body, every atom in your body, even the smallest part of your body that you can conceive is exactly the same as the light, and that the entire body has disappeared in the light.

"That is right Milon, you are the light. The light is you, and the light is your infinite consciousness, Milon."

Milon was ablaze, and at one with the light.

"Allow the light to expand, Milon. Let it expand to fill this entire room. The whole area. The entire city. County. State. The light remaining infinite expands to fill the entire land. The light expands to fill the country."

Milon's boundaries began to melt as the Wizard continued, "The light expands to fill the entire continent, the light expands to fill the other continents. Expanding to fill the entire planet — out past the moon and solar system. The light expands to fill the the entire galaxy. Other galaxies. All galaxies. The entire universe. The light expands to the entire known and unknown universe."

Milon's consciousness, fully expanded, was at one with the universe.

"And Milon," continued the Wizard, "now notice that the light, remaining infinite, is all contained in your body, which has become hollow to accommodate it. You are the light, Milon, the light is you.

"Very Good, Milon. The light knows your purpose. The light knows your purpose in this lifetime. I want the light to tell you your purpose, and to tell either your conscious mind or your unconscious mind. So you may hear it consciously or unconsciously. Have the light tell you your purpose. Do that now."

The Wizard waited. Milon, who had been for several minutes just infinite light, noticed something happening just outside of his awareness.

The Wizard continued. "If the light is only telling your unconscious mind, could I please suggest that your unconscious mind set up some symbol, or something that which for you will represent your purpose.

And if it is your conscious mind, have the symbol represent your purpose, so that you can know your purpose, symbolically."

Milon saw a symbol appear in his mind, and then he heard the words. No one had spoken them, but he heard the words as clearly as if you had spoken them to him, and they said, "Milon, your purpose is to know that you can create your own future, and to share that knowledge with others." Tears began to stream down Milon's face. It felt so good to know his purpose, and who he was. He was crying as the Wizard said, "Good. And now, come back from the light."

Milon didn't want to, not really, and he was about to tell the Wizard, as he heard as if from a long way away, "I know you may not want to. It's all right, because the light is there and you know where it is. You can visit the light anytime you want, because you are the light and the light is you.

"Since there is more to do," said the Wizard, "Please come back from the light and stand on the future end of your Time Line and hold your hands out in front of you and allow the beams of light to flow from your fingers all the way down through your Time Line through now."

Milon was standing on the future end of his Time Line, and light was streaming from his outstretched hands. The beams of light streamed out of his hands, but the infinite light in his body was not diminished. And as he did, his Time Line began to glow.

The Wizard continued, "And notice that your Time Line is infused with the purpose of life — your purpose.

"Take all the time you need," said the Wizard, "you've got it. Take all the time you need to allow your future to be totally infused with the light of your purpose."

The Wizard waited as Milon's Time Line began to glow even more brightly. "Excellent," he said, "And as you move toward now, notice how good it feels and notice all the changes that have occurred inside you and your ability to know your purpose, and be able to have exactly what it is that you want."

"Now that you mention it," thought Milon.

"That's right," the Wizard said. "And what I'd like you to do now is, I'd like you to come slowly back toward now, only as quickly as all the events between then and now re-evaluate themselves in light of your purpose and your newfound capabilities. Your capabilities of having whatever it is that you want, your capabilities of being able to learn whatever it is you need to learn to have whatever it is you want to have. The capabilities of your unconscious mind providing to you the information that you need to be able to do whatever it is you want to do, and have any recall you need in order to be able to use what you've learned in ways that will totally support you.

"Allow it to occur in the future, in your present or in your past, wherever the change is needed, let it happen. Take all the time you need, as you slowly come back toward now. Notice that all the events in your Time Line are totally realigning themselves, and re-evaluating themselves.

"When you get to now, just float right down into now."

Milon blinked, and rubbed his eyes sleepily. The room looked different. The Wizard continued, "As you slowly open your eyes, not yet, but when you do slowly open your eyes, notice that the room looks just a little bit different that when you left. Notice that when you look at it, the table, chairs, even the window next to you looks different than they did a moment ago. I'd like you to notice that your body feels just a little bit different, too. In fact, the kinds of things you're feeling are perfectly appropriate, for the new you."

Milon was in awe. The room seemed aglow. His body felt light, and a little tingly, almost as if it were not there all the way.

"I'd like you to notice as you slowly awake that you become more and more awake. Take all the time you need of course, to do that, but as you do, I'd like you to notice that between now and this evening, that you have all the time you need to enjoy all the things that you will. I'd like you to notice that before you leave the room, not yet, but before you leave the room, that you're actually fully wide awake, and it may surprise you just how much energy you have for the rest of the day. In fact, it may be surprising for you to notice that you have even more energy than you thought. You will have a lot of energy until it's time to fall asleep tonight, at which point you will fall into a very deep sleep, and the integration we started here, completes itself, while you sleep tonight.

"In the past, Milon, you have contacted me in your mind," said the Wizard. "I am there, Milon, but that is no longer necessary for us to talk in this manner. You know 'the Process.' Now you can trust yourself. This is a new beginning for you, Milon. To take the next step Milon, you must be one with the information and practices. The ones I have taught you so far. Review them, Milon, and every time you do, you will notice tremendous gains.

"Review in cycles, Milon, once a day for one week.

Then once a month for three months.

"The first review cycle will bring you to the level of understanding the secrets of the universe — the ability to tap into the universe, and create anything you want in the material world.

"The second cycle will allow you to become at one with yourself and with your brothers in the world. During this cycle, Milon, you will find the spirituality you seek, and the closeness with your brothers and sisters.

"The third review cycle, Milon, will bring you to the level of being able to affect the planet on a global level.

"The fourth, will bring you to the vision state, Milon. This is where you may know what you want, just by willing it.

"And when you are ready, you may come and study with me," said the Wizard.

"You do understand, do you not?"

"I understand," said Milon with tears of gratitude streaming down his face. "Now, I understand. Thank-you."

"Good," said the Wizard. "If you need me, until you are ready to come and study with me, I am in the light." And he turned and walked into the white light. The Wizard's body disappeared as he became one with the light.

Milon, with tears of joy still wet on his face, opened the notebook the Wizard had given him. He knew what he wanted. He knew how to get it. He knew what to do, and what he wanted to do NOW was to become the Wizard.

Appendix

FREE POCKET CARD

Send for your free pocket card. The card will help to remind you of what you have learned. The card is designed to fit neatly in your wallet or purse. The card includes:

The Seven Frames
The Five Principles
The Prosperity Beliefs

It will serve as a friendly reminder to help you create your own success, throughout your future. And it is free on request. Call the number or write to the address on the following order form. Include your name and address with your request.

THE SECRET OF CREATING YOUR FUTURE™ PERSONAL SUCCESS PROGRAM

with Tad James

12 audios, 1 VHS video, Personal Success Guide, $119.95

You, too, can go through the process of Creating Your Future®. Put these powerful principles to work to enhance your life and design your destiny. Now you can actually experience this life-changing process, masterly guided by Dr. Tad James. You'll learn these 12 amazing secrets:

1. YOUR OWN INTERNAL TIME MACHINE
Discover your internal time machine, or Time Line, and how it creates the future.

2. GET BACK IN TOUCH WITH YOUR DREAMS
Have you ever sold out on your dreams, and settled for something less? Rediscover the dreams you had when you were younger, so you won't ever have to sell out again. Once you've done this, you'll be back in touch with what you dreamed, and well on the way to deciding if you really want it.

3. HOW NEGATIVE EMOTIONS KEEP YOU FROM YOUR DREAMS
Learn all about negative emotions, and how they interfere with you having what you want. You don't have to learn to live with them, you only have to release them using this incredible yet simple process, quickly and easily.

4. DESTROYING YOUR ANGER
Get rid of any anger. Anger can keep you from having the kind of future you want. Finally you can release the anger from the events from the past, and preserve any learnings that were necessary. Once you do this, anger will no longer block your progress, and keep you from having what you want in your future.

5. ELIMINATE THE DESTRUCTIVE POWER OF GUILT
Discover how guilt keeps you from creating your future, and learn three new ways to look at your past actions. This will allow you to know for certain that you've learned from past events. Then, wherever appropriate, you can release the guilt from past memories, so that guilt from your past isn't interfering with you having what you want.

6. LIVING WITHOUT SADNESS
Sadness doesn't make it easier for us to achieve what we want in the future. It only makes it more difficult. Discover how to release all your

sadness, and learn about alternative ways to deal with sadness from the past that's holding you back. Then, you may find that the sadness that you felt in the past just isn't an issue any more, and that you have a way to deal with all the sadness that may come up in the future. In any case, you'll be far more able to create your future the way you want it.

7. MOVING FROM FEAR TO POWER
Fear stops you from doing an awful lot of things that you could or should be doing, and now you'll discover some alternate ways of dealing with your fears, and how to release those fears that don't support you. After using a simple technique you will have released fear from the events from the past, and preserved any learnings and protection that were necessary in the process. Fear will no longer block your progress, and keep you from creating your future.

8. TOTAL EMOTIONAL FREEDOM FOREVER
Clear any other emotions that block you from having what you want. Use this wonderful process to keep yourself clear in the future, should you need to.

9. THE KEY TO MAKING THE RIGHT DECISIONS IN LIFE
If you're like most people, you've made decisions in the past that limit you today, but how do you overcome them? Discover how to clear out any limiting decisions you made in the past that keep you from having what you want. You'll learn how limiting decisions block future success, and how to clear them out very quickly and easily.

10. THE SECRET TO BEING MOTIVATED ALL THE TIME
Values are the key to all motivation. Get some real clarity on what your values really are, and how to use them so they support your dreams. Then, use some very advanced methods for clearing out any conflicts that make you incongruent or wishy-washy about the future. Get an empowering new perspective over your life that you've never had before.

11. BRINGING YOUR DREAMS TO LIFE NOW!
And now we get to the meat of **The Secret of Creating Your Future™**. This valuable insight will give you new certainty about how to create what you want in your life.

12. FINALLY LIVING THE LIFE YOU'VE ALWAYS DREAMED OF
This final secret to Creating your Future® is probably the most powerful method for actualizing your dreams. You can have what you want, when you want, with truly amazing consistency. You'll treasure this invaluable technique.

TIME LINE THERAPY™ & THE BASIS OF PERSONALITY

by Tad James & Wyatt Woodsmall
Paperback, $27.95

Many people say this is one of the most important NLP books written to date. In it is a study of the most important elements that make up a person's core personality. Those elements include:

- **Time Line** - - Memory Storage. Introduction, understanding the two types, discovering your time line, memory management, the language of time, handling trauma, programming your future, Time Line Therapy outline.
- **Meta Programs** - - Unconscious Filters of Perception. Introduction, understanding simple and complex meta programs, changing meta programs.
- **Values** - - The Key to Motivation. Introduction, formation of values, evolution of values, resolving beliefs and values conflicts, changing values.
- Changing the Basis of Personality

This book is a must for every student of NLP or human change technologies. The contents of the book is so important that it is required reading and reference for all our NLP certification courses, basic and advanced.
(ISBN 0-916990-21-4)

THE SECRET OF CREATING YOUR FUTURE

by Tad James
Paperback, $9.95

Share the secret with people you care about. A great gift for friends or family. If you are a therapist or counselor, use this book as a tool for your clients. Help your clients gain greater control over their lives. Make this book available to them.
(ISBN 0-9623272-0-4)

PROMETHEUS INDUCTION

with Tad James

1 Induction Tape, $16.95

Due to the successful results people have been reporting about A Journey on the Time Line, Tad created this new induction tape. Also known as the Time Line Project Induction, this is a very powerful closed-eye process. It was created to assist you to:

- Connect with the people or resources you may need to complete a specific project or achieve a desired goal.
- Increase your energy for your project.
- Resolve Time Line issues which may hamper your success.

A Time Line Elicitation is included for those who need help determining how their time line is arranged.

A JOURNEY ON THE TIME LINE

with Tad James

1 Induction Tape, $16.95

Experience the effectiveness of Time Line Therapy™ with this personal induction. Take a guided journey into the past and out into the future. Especially designed to integrate learning and tap inner resources. Enhances communication between your conscious mind and your unconscious mind. Includes a Time Line Elicitation to help you discover exactly how your time line is arranged.

THE NLP PRACTITIONER TRAINING COLLECTION

with Tad James

24 audio cassettes, manual, $425

The NLP Practitioner Training Collection brings a full NLP Practitioner Course into your car or home, allowing you to immediately experience the powerful basic principles and techniques of neuro-linguistic programming. This package is a convenient and economical solution for those unable to invest in a live certification course at this time, yet know the many benefits of such training. Advanced training techniques and effective demonstration of what is taught make learning and using this information easy, enjoyable and rewarding. Great review program for Certified NLP practitioners or NLP trainers.

FOCUS OF APPLICATIONS:

- Business and Sales
- Personal Growth and Change
- Therapy and Relationships
- Education and Learning

MAIN TOPICS:

- Introduction to NLP
- Submodalities
- Strategies
- Anchoring & Reframing
- Sensory Acuity
- Rapport & Rep Systems
- Language Patterns
- Basic Time Line Therapy™

Includes 24 audios, manual and certificate of completion.

TIME LINE THERAPY™ VIDEO COURSE

with Tad James

4 videos, 4 audios, manual, $295

This advanced NLP training offers comprehensive instruction on how to use Tad's Time Line Therapy™ model for quick, long lasting change.

With applications for therapy, business & personal development, this program will allow you to discover, learn & experience:

- Elicitation of an individual's Time Line.
- How memories are arranged on the Time Line
- Changing personal history with Time Line including guilt, anxiety, negative emotions, limiting decisions, trauma & phobias.
- Cleaning up internal conflicts using parts integration, values

integration & family alignment.

- Other Time Line healing techniques.
- Changing the Time Line.
- Programming Your Future.
- And other recent developments by Tad.

Nice quality, professionally edited production. Includes 4 edited videos, 4 audios, manual and certificate of completion.

ERICKSONIAN HYPNOSIS VIDEO COURSE

with Tad James

4 videos, 5 audios, manual, $295

Discover the world of the unconscious mind. Tad has researched almost all of Milton Erickson's facinating work. He has also been doing major research in the historic works on hypnosis and integrating it with recent developments like Time Line Therapy™ and NLP. This deep knowledge of the subject allows Tad to make powerful new connections with the latest research in accelerated behavioral change.

Topics covered include:

- Advanced hypnotic language patterns.
- Verbal & non-verbal suggestion.
- Direct & indirect suggestion.
- Methods of trance induction.
- Hypnotic rapport.
- Utilizing naturally occurring trance.
- The real history of NLP.
- History of hypnosis.
- Utilization & linkage.
- Sources for further study & more.

Nice quality, professionally edited production. Includes 4 edited videos, 5 audios, manual and certificate of completion.

Money Back Guarantee of Satisfaction

We want you to be satisfied and richly rewarded for placing your confidence with us. All books and tapes we offer are completely guaranteed. If you are not completely satisfied with your order, you have the privilege of returning it for a refund of the purchase price.

TIME LINE THERAPY ASSOCIATION, INC.

Time Line Therapy™ is recognized as one of the most useful techniques for helping people change quickly and easily. If youwish to use Time Line Therapy™ techniques for more than your own personal growth, we recommend proper training. The Time Line Therapy™ Association was established to promote the use and training of these techniques and establish ethical guidelines for it's use. For information on approved Time Line Therapy™ training centers, contact:

615 Pi'ikoi Street, Suite 501
Honolulu, Hawaii 96814 USA
Telephone (808) 596-7765 • Fax: (808) 596-7764
e-mail: tlta@hypnosis.com

ORDER FORM

Send your request to:

Advanced Neuro Dynamics-CYF
615 Piikoi Street, Suite 501 l Honolulu, HI 96814 USA
e-mail: info@nlp.com
website: www.nlp.com

Credit Card Orders can call toll free from the U.S. & Canada:
(800) 800-MIND • Direct (808) 596-7765 • Fax (808) 596-7764

Name ______________________________

Address ______________________________

City/State ____________________ Zip __________

Phone ______________________________

Qty	Item	Price
____	Free Catalog of Books, Tapes & Seminars	FREE
____	....	FREE
____	**The Secret of Creating Your Future**, by Tad James, ...	$9.95
____	**Time Line Therapy & The Basis of Personality,** by James & Woodsmall. Cloth. (1.5 lb.) (0-916990-21-4)	$24.95
____	**A Journey On the Time Line,** with Tad James (0.5 lb.)	$16.95
____	**Time Line Project Induction,** with Tad James. (0.5 lb.)	$16.95
____	**The Secret of Creating Your Future** (audio) (3.5 lb.)	$119.95
____	**Time Line Therapy™ Video Course** (8.0 lb.)	$295.00
____	**Ericksonian Hypnosis Video Course** (8.0 lb.)	$295.00
____	**NLP Practitioner Training Collection,** with Tad James. (8.0 lb.)	$425.00

Sub Total: __________

Hawaii residents add 4.167% tax: __________

Weight (lbs.): __________ **Shipping** (from table below): __________

Total (U.S. funds only): __________

Indicate Method of Payment:

❏ Check ❏ Money Order ❏ VISA ❏ MasterCard ❏ AMEX

Card No: ____________________ Exp: __________

Air Shipping
Shipping charge is equal to the handing fee plus postage per pound. Round postage up to nearest pound. (Subject to rate increases.)

Destination	Handling	Postage Per Lb.
To USA	$3.00	$1.50
To Canada	$6.50	$1.75
To all Other	$9.00	$5.75